INTERPRETING CHILDREN'S DRAWINGS

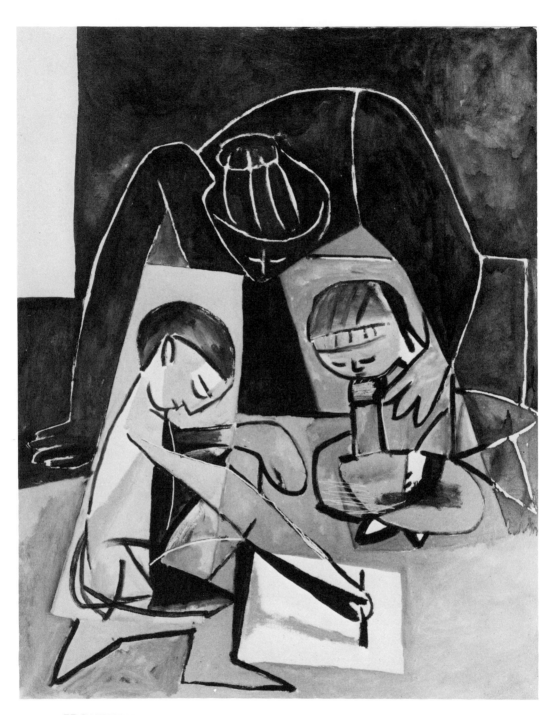

FRONTISPIECE

Picasso. Claude dessinant. HP 209 Musée Picasso. © SPADEM, Paris/VAGA, New York, 1981.

INTERPRETING CHILDREN'S DRAWINGS

by

JOSEPH H. DI LEO, M.D.

BRUNNER/MAZEL Publishers · New York

Third Printing

Library of Congress Cataloging in Publication Data

Di Leo, Joseph H., 1902–
  Interpreting children's drawings.

  Bibliography: p.
  Includes indexes.
  1. Drawing, Psychology of. 2. Art and mental illness.
3. Child psychology. I. Title. [DNLM: 1. Affective
symptoms—Diagnosis. 2. Affective symptoms—In infancy
and childhood. 3. Art 4. Projective technics—In
infancy and childhood. WS 105.5.E8 D576i]
BF723.D7D48   1983   618.92'89075   83-2516
ISBN 0-87630-327-0
ISBN 0-87630-331-9 (pbk.)

Published by

BRUNNER/MAZEL, INC.
19 Union Square West
New York, New York 10003

Contents

Plates and Acknowledgments

Frontispiece. PICASSO: Claude dessinant. HP 209. Musée Picasso. © SPADEM Paris/VAGA, New York, 1981.

Plate I. LACHAISE, G: *Floating Figure* (1927). Museum of Modern Art, New York.

Plate II. VINCI, Leonardo da: Inv. No. #12276 Verso. The Royal Library, Windsor Castle. Copyright reserved.

Plate III. WÖLFLI, A: Riesen-Stadt, Waaben-Hall. 1917. Inv. 1964. 80. Copyright owner Kunstmuseum Basel, Kupferstichkabinett.

My acknowledgments are gratefully made to the Directors and Curators of the museums and library listed above for permission to reproduce works of art in their collections.

I wish to express my deeply felt gratitude to Sister Theresa Kelly of the New York Foundling Hospital and to her assistant, Ms. Debbie Decker, for their generous cooperation.

Very special thanks go to the hundreds of young persons who have shared with me their thoughts, feelings, and aspirations.

Thanks are also due to Giulio Einaudi Editore, Torino, and to the author for permission to reproduce the drawings from *Il Complesso di Laio* by T. Giani Gallino.

Preface

This work was originally intended as an extension of my earlier volume and I had, in fact, thought to call it *Children's Drawings as Diagnostic Aids II*. The preponderance of new material, however, warrants a new title, though not a new approach, for it remains my contention that the addition of pieces of information such as may be derived from statistical analysis does not constitute a whole. The concept may be shopworn but it is nonetheless vital, and bears repetition, that the whole is an entity greater than the sum of its component parts. It is accordingly with that concept in mind that the drawings will be viewed and interpreted clinically.

This book is without polemical intent. Quite the contrary. I shall borrow freely from various sources. I appreciate the laudable efforts of investigators who apply the methods of science to all aspects of human behavior including drawings; but the information currently available from these studies is insufficient to eliminate the subjective variable in interpretation. It is necessary to be constantly aware that the drawings are aids and should be but a part of a general diagnostic and therapeutic procedure; they may assist but not replace the clinician.

Among material treated not at all or insufficiently in my earlier works are chapters on changing sex roles, laterality, global and atomistic features, similarities and differences between the drawings of normal children and regressed adults, tree drawings, effects of family pathology. More extensive and deeper insights are offered in interpreting expressions of cognition and emotion. A chapter is devoted to the drawing of a house, its symbolism, and the child's perception of it as fulfilling its role as haven.

As a main focus, I have selected the developmental phase that Sigmund Freud intuitively named "latency," when the energy derived from sexual impulses is often diverted to social and intellectual pursuits. Apparently dormant, these impulses will erupt with renewed vigor when a shower of hormones results in physical changes and new desires that cannot be ignored.

The role of biological and cultural factors in the diminution of overt sexual drive during latency remains unresolved, while the role of protagonist seems to be undergoing a theoretical shift from child back to parent—from Oedipus to Laius—a return to the original position of Freud before he made the crucial decision to abandon the seduction theory in favor of infantile sexuality.

But what is so special about latency-age children to merit the impressive attention they have been getting? Working directly with children, Anna Freud in particular, as well as other prominent investigators, have greatly facilitated our understanding of latency in its relation to ego development, hormonal effects, aggression, industry, and diminution of egocentricity. The apparent equilibrium of the phase obscures underlying phenomena that are, nonetheless, actively at work, notably the infantile and preadolescent intrusions at opposite ends of the phase. No area of the developmental spectrum can be isolated as though there were no past or future, for here, too, in Shakespeare's words, " . . . what's past is prologue, what to come. . . . " Accordingly, latency has a backward reference into early childhood, and a forward reference into adolescence and adulthood. I shall make excursions into both areas to broaden the perspective.

During the 33 years that I served as Director of the Developmental Clinic at New York Foundling Hospital, my work was with individual children. Much of my time was set aside for a study of their drawings, an activity that continues to fascinate me, for in them lies a rich fount of information that has immeasurably enhanced my understanding of individual children and, I might add, of many adults. Fashions and attitudes change but the child is ever father to the man.

Many of the problems besetting children and their families are manifesting themselves with distressingly increasing frequency during the years when conflicts are supposed to be dormant, while social activities, sports, and learning are enjoyed. Thus, a study of drawings may tell why a given child is acting out while others are sublimating. Often, the anger, void, and unhappiness repressed from verbal expression are freely externalized in graphic activity well before the struggle for containment may bow to the overpowering demands of adolescence.

Each unhappy child is so in a very personal way. Facts are meaningless until we put into them something of our own. A clinical approach helps to free the mind from what Norman Cousins has called "the overworked tendency to think statistically."

1

INTERPRETATION

"that I may see and tell
of things invisible to mortal sight."
John Milton

Hard data and soft signs

To interpret: to bring out the meaning.

In a quest for meanings, the searcher may fruitfully pursue more than one path. More satisfying to the scientifically oriented mind is the gathering of hard facts that can be subjected to statistical analysis and tested for reliability and validity. In the study of drawings, this method is used to establish the degree to which a given finding correlates with a significance that has been attributed to it. Is the emphasis on hands related to aggressive tendencies? A general statement in the affirmative may be justified when the item is encountered in a significantly large number of aggressive persons.

Another approach available to the investigator lies in a longitudinal, in-depth study of single persons who exhibit huge hands consistently in their drawings along with aggression as a consistent feature of their behavior. This clinical approach will be all the more convincing if follow-up reveals concomitant reduction of hand size and aggressive behavior.

In a combination of the two approaches, piecemeal hard data attain greater validity within a confirmatory global perception. Such holistic interpretation is more likely to appeal to clinicians and accounts for the widespread use of drawings in clinical diagnosis and therapy.

For the moment, I shall limit myself to a bare statement that will be dealt with more pervasively throughout this book, to wit: in the present state of our knowledge, interpretation of child art cannot validly shed the human element of subjectivity; statistical evidence alone is limited in scope and insufficiently conclusive to preclude conflicting views.

Interpretation can be aided by taking into account general trends as indicated by statistical studies. But understanding of children can be achieved only by studying them as individuals, since no two are alike.

Drawings are one means of establishing a rapid, easy, pleasant rapport with the child. Among clinicians, Winnicott is especially notable for his Squiggle Game in which he exploited to the fullest the first crucial therapeutic interview by engaging the child in an exchange of drawings reciprocally suggested and completed. The child plays an active role in his own analysis. At the discretion of the analyst, the drawings may be shown to the parents. Those who have used drawings in their work with children know how amazed parents can be when shown in graphic terms how their child perceives them and sees Self in relation to the family.

The subjective element in interpretation is inherent in the individual doing the interpretation. Just as no two children are alike, no two professionals are alike. My experience of over three decades has dispelled any notion of dogmatic interpretation. The reader may view the material I am about to present in a different light and disagree or see beyond my interpretation.

In any case, beyond question is the potential value of drawings for those who work with children, the mentally or emotionally disabled of all ages, or where there is a language barrier.

The role of speech in interpretation of drawings

Articulate children are likely to talk as they draw. These comments should be noted as they may clarify what may not be visibly evident.

In preschool children, however, the original idea may be to draw, let us say, a cat; but as the figure is developed, it may undergo a series of appellations, as it is labeled car or boat. On the following day, the same child is shown the drawing and insists that it is a house. In school-age children, one expects greater consistency between graphic product and the spoken word.

I believe that children should be encouraged to tell what they are doing or have drawn, but in a general way. By asking specifically, "What is it?", we shall be obliged with a reply that may be unrelated to the drawing. It is better to listen or at most to say something nonspecific such as, "Tell me something about it."

Any comment that the child makes when shown a drawing may be a clue to attitude, thought, or feeling. In this connection, I am reminded that back in 1913 Luquet tells how, in drawing with ink, children might accidentally make a blot; unperturbed, as though made intentionally, they would call it a dog or an ocean, or whatever (Rorschach's *Psychodiagnostics* appeared in 1942).

In young children, the superiority of speech over drawing as a means of communication is only apparent. By the time the child begins to draw a recognizable figure, speech is well advanced in the sense that innumerable words have been added to the vocabulary as sentences become longer and syntactically correct. Yet, this discrepancy between speech and drawing may create a false impression. Better than speech, drawings may express a subtlety of intellect and affect that is beyond the power or freedom of verbal expression. Even the adult, with a formidable vocabulary, requires hundreds of words in an attempt to convey what a picture can do at once. Literary skill alone cannot create a mental image that will precisely evoke the actual appearance of the object described—unless one is a John Keats before a Grecian urn. The written or spoken word can interpret and comment upon the image before the viewer but not satisfactorily replace it. Therein lies the respect accorded the work of children by those who would understand and heal them.

Despite the reservations one may have regarding the relevancy of verbal comments by young children, they should be encouraged to talk while the examiner, avoiding suggestion, listens and notes. School-age children may contribute to interpretation by providing the associations and context. The drawing is a personal expression and so is its meaning.

A developmental perspective

A valid appraisal of any aspect of behavior must take into due account the subject's age and developmental level. This general rule applies with particular cogency to children. It is essential to know what to expect as the child matures. A formidable body of research has identified significant attainments or milestones along the way. Stage-dependent theories (Freud, Erikson, Piaget, Gesell) have facilitated our understanding of the developmental process. The present writer has devised a synoptic chart in which stage-dependent theories and facts are integrated so as to present a holistic view from birth to adolescence (Di Leo, 1977).

Depending upon the child's developmental age, the presence or absence of parts of the human figure may have a conceptual or an affective meaning as in the following instances:

> Fact: A female figure shows the lower part of the body through the clothing.
>
> Interpretation: Depends upon maturity of the artist. Preschool children commonly resort to X-ray technique, as they draw what they know to be there regardless of whether it is actually visible. Intellectual realism of the preoperational child. School-age prepubertal child drawing transparencies suggests mental disability or function below age-level expectations. Possibly a suggestion of seduction as in Figure 1 by a girl age 8 years 11 months. If drawn by an adolescent or adult, transparency of the lower part of the figure is indicative of voyeuristic tendency.

Many errors in interpretation occur because of lack of familiarity with what is usual at various levels of developmental age.

FIGURE 1

By girl, age 8 years 11 months. Transparency through skirt, drawn as an afterthought, possibly to make the figure more seductive.

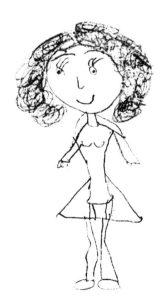

Emphasis on buttons has been noted in drawings by maladjusted persons, especially those whose behavior indicates mother-dependence (Machover, 1949).

In Figure 2, a girl of 6 years 6 months has drawn her father. Buttons are a conspicuous feature of his attire. Granted that they do symbolize dependency, I can see no significance beyond the usual attachment of girls her age to their fathers. What child is independent at age 6?

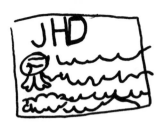

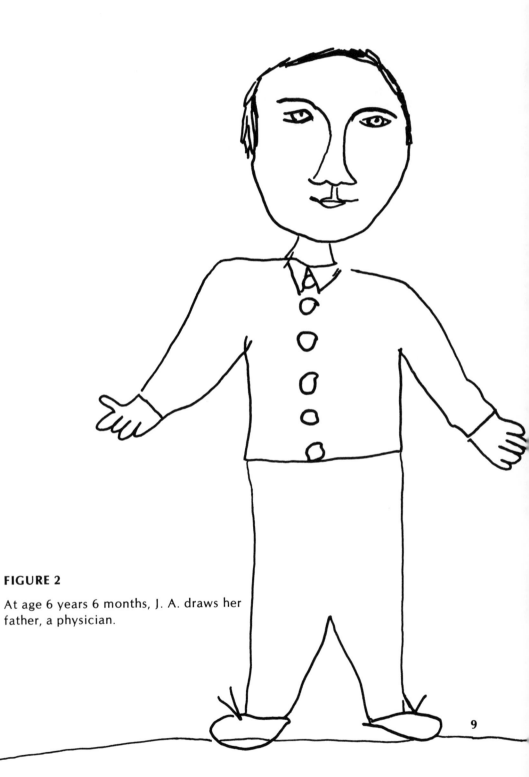

FIGURE 2

At age 6 years 6 months, J. A. draws her
father, a physician.

9

But then we have Figure 3 in which a girl of 11 years has drawn a self-portrait (she called it "me," indicating herself). The arms and neck are heavily shaded (anxiety). There is an interminable double row of buttons irrelevantly placed down one side, and a pocket over the breast area. The girl is under treatment for a seizure disorder. Her school work is poor to a degree that has resulted in her transfer to an ungraded class. She is aware of her deficiencies, is totally lacking in motivation, and feels quite inadequate. Her difficulties are aggravated by feelings of rejection stemming from her father's frequent referral to her as "stupid." In this preadolescent child, the exaggerated emphasis on buttons, the pocket, the shading, and above all, the global impression conveyed by this strange figure may very well express a personality that is dependent, infantile, and inadequate. This interpretation is supported by the clinical findings.

FIGURE 3

Drawn by a girl of 11 years.

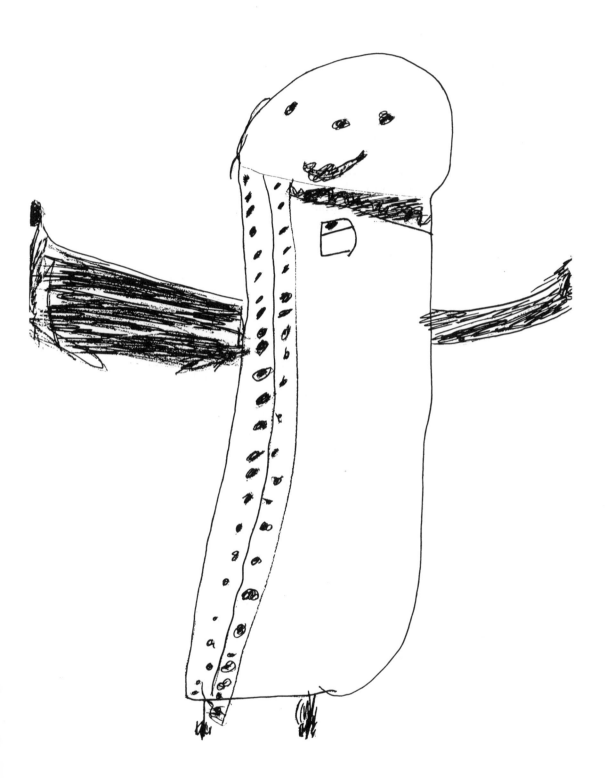

Symbols

The advent of civilized humans has been related to the invention of script some four thousand years ago. Yet, cave paintings at Altamira and Lascaux attest to the human need to represent graphically the objects of interest, and thereby to possess them at least in their image, some twenty or thirty thousand years ago.

Symbols are the most general and effective means of communication. An object may signify an abstract entity, as does the gentle dove representing peace, by widespread conscious consent. Or, a symbol may surface from the cauldron of archetypes in a dream or graphically in the form of a mandala. Then again, the object may be transitional bridging the gap between the inner world and the reality outside one's self, as does the object that the child takes to bed for company (Winnicott, 1971). All these forms are seen in child art.

Just as the manifest content of a dream becomes meaningful when related to the dreamer's personal associations, so too do the symbols, consciously or unconsciously drawn, achieve meaning only when viewed within the context of the maker's personal history. The symbol may not have the same meaning for different persons. A drawing showing someone falling in water has a special significance if made by an alcoholic. The content of a drawing tells something about the person; the nature of the person tells something about the drawing.

Specific items in a drawing gain validity when referred to the whole drawing. And this in turn gains validity when considered as an element in a comprehensive diagnostic evaluation.

In drawings, as in dreams, the recurrence of a theme and its symbols is a noteworthy phenomenon. It may be the expression of an important event, traumatic, or impressive in any case, breaking through the repressive barrier.

That is another reason, besides the opportunity for comparison with previous drawings, why serial specimens should be obtained when possible. The drawings become permanent documents which illustrate at a glance the changes that have occurred over a period of time.

Jung (1968) emphasizes a basic difference between sign and symbol. The sign is man-made. Meaningless in itself, it stands by common consent for an object or an instruction such as the stop and go traffic sign. A symbol is basically quite different. It is a natural spontaneous phenomenon whose meaning is hidden beneath its obvious form. In contrast to the sign, it represents more than is apparent. Dreams and unconscious thoughts, feelings, and actions are sources of symbols. These require interpretation within the context of the only reality: the person who dreams, acts, or draws. The key in lock is one of the more commonly interpreted symbols of sexual intercourse. Yet even in Italy, where the key itself is designated as male or female accordingly as it is solid to push or hollow to receive (chiave maschia, chiave femmina), I doubt such unconscious messages arrive whenever people reenter their homes.

Nowhere has symbolism attained greater refinement than in the visual arts of India and China. The aim of this art was to convey an appreciation of spiritual, abstract ideas through the medium of physical attributes.

It was at first believed impossible to represent the Buddha, since with Nirvana he had attained extinction. Later on, it was felt that the faithful required some physical stimulus to their veneration, so it was decided to represent "the Enlightened One" by a huge symbolic footstep that graved in stone would attest to his grandeur. Eventually, under the influence of Hellenistic artists, the Buddha was given anthropomorphic representation. This was governed by a minutely described list of 32 sacred marks (lakṣanā) by which he could be identified. Among these are the cranial protuberance (iṣṇiṣa), the mystic smile of peaceful meditation, and the curl between the eye-brows (ūrṇā). Another striking feature of all images are the large ears with greatly elongated ear lobes. A repertory of hand and finger gestures (mudras) express protection, meditation, prayer, teaching, and other functions of the Buddha.

The mandala (Sanscrit "circle") appears frequently in Buddhist iconography, both as a holy precinct around the Buddha and as a representation of the cosmos. The mandala is not peculiar to any particular culture. It is found universally to denote wholeness. It is the beginning of all representational art. In the lives of all of us it marked the astounding moment when, in a casually drawn circle, we recognized something in our environment, perhaps a head. We had made our first symbol. We then went on to deliberately use the figure to represent eyes, mouth, and nose within the primordial circle. We added rays to make the sun, as did our remotest forbears, and as do our sisters and brothers all over the globe.

Universality of the phenomenon led Jung to regard the mandala as an archetypal symbol reflecting the common neuropsychological inheritance of humankind.

The use of space

For purposes of analysis, the space on which the person or tree is to be drawn may be divided by a transverse imaginary line into an upper and lower half, and by a vertical line into a right and left half. There is general support for the view that small figures drawn at or near the lower edge express feelings of inadequacy, insecurity, even depression, while those in the upper half suggest optimism, perhaps narcissism, and fantasy.

Placement to the right or left of the midline is interpreted in a variety of ways. To begin with, one is faced with determining whether the right and left are those of the viewer or the viewed. Then one needs to consider cultural directionality in writing from left to right or vice-versa, as this may bear upon the side one habitually starts to write, perhaps to draw. For purposes of this discussion, let us assume that the subject has been taught to write from left to right and that the right and left of the page are those of the viewer.

According to Buck (1974), placement of the figure away from the mid-axis, to the left, occurs in impulsive subjects likely to seek emotional satisfaction. Those whose figure is far to the right are frequently reflective persons who are likely to wait for intellectual satisfaction. Machover (1949) regarded placement to the left as indicating a personality that is self-oriented, in contrast to the environmentally-oriented who tend to place the figure on the right side of the page. Most well-adjusted persons will draw the figure well centered, not strikingly small or huge.

In her treatise on trees, Bolander (1977), in addition to the interpretations that apply to person drawings, unequivocally assigns sexual significance to the left and right sides of the page. She regards the left as the female principle; the right, the male. The tree that tilts to one side or the other expresses father or mother influence as predominant. Bolander also interprets the upper half of the page as the area of the future, the present represented by the center, and the lower half as the zone that comprises the past.

Buck (1974) views placement towards the left as indicative of impulsive, emotional, self-centered tendencies; placement towards the right suggests controlled tendencies and an inclination to seek intellectual rather than emotional satisfaction. Though conceding that there is evidence for believing the left to be the feminine side and the right the masculine, Buck regards this as a dubious point.

Secure latency-age children, free from inhibiting anxiety, give unrestricted rein to fantasy, as in this drawing by Alfred, age 7 years 9 months (Figure 4).

In an elaborate and imaginative drawing, he has depicted a lively maritime scene. One sailor is drinking and hiccupping; the other is yelling "dlog, dlog" (gold, gold), having discovered a treasure chest. Meanwhile, a swordfish is pointing for the submerged part of the hull. All this takes place under a smiling sun.

Obviously, this is a freely expressed fantasy by a bright child.

Additional significance will become apparent if the page is divid-

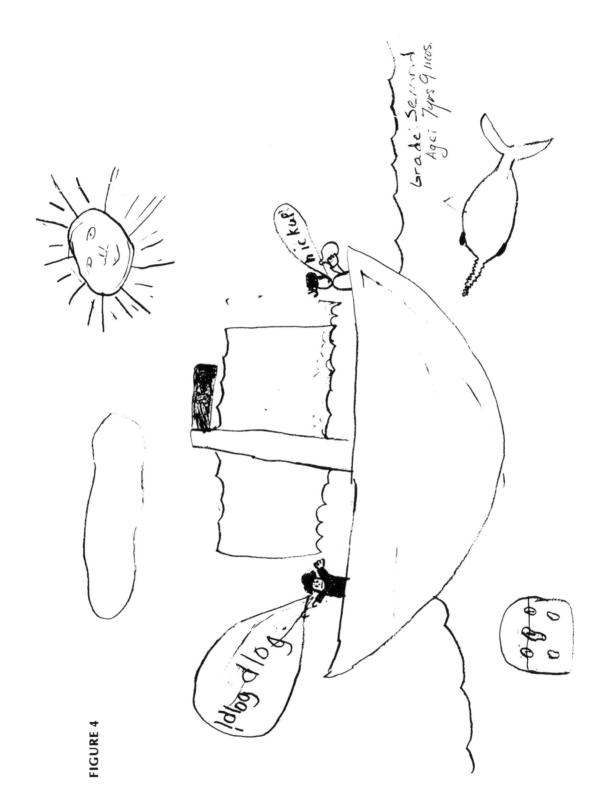

FIGURE 4

ed into two halves by an imaginary line running down the middle. On the right (male) side, there is a male symbol, a sword, about to penetrate the ship (female). There is also a liquor-imbibing sailor on that side. On the left (female) side, there is another female symbol, the chest with its gold. The boy's perception of sex roles is unconsciously portrayed.

Power (the sun) shines from the right. Evil forces, alcoholism, and aggression are also on that side. The treasure chest is good; it is on the left.

The artist is not a mirror writer; he has reversed the word "gold" as a code.

2

FORMAL AND STYLISTIC ATTRIBUTES

Quality of line

In addition to manifest content and symbolism, feeling states find expression in lines, use of space, balance, integration, and manner of execution.

A figure drawn with light, wavering, broken lines speaks for an insecure, depressed child. Conversely, the bold, continual, freely drawn figure is expressive of self-confidence and a feeling of security. The first is hesitant, appears to think as he goes along. The second seems to be carrying out what is already clearly visualized as the hand obeys the intellect.*

---

*I have observed drawing with a continual unbroken line made without lifting pencil from paper in work by seriously disturbed children. It has been noted by others that artistic ability and emotional disorder may coexist.

FIGURE 5

By Kenneth, age 12. Lines are unbroken and boldly drawn. The figure is a square-jawed, muscular male.

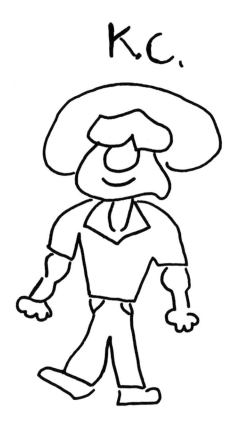

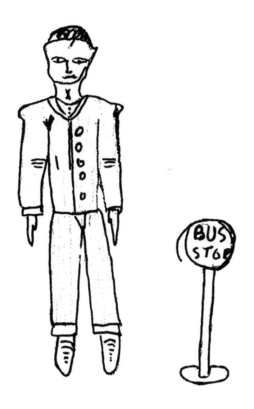

FIGURE 6

By Sandro, age 11. Intelligent. Timid. Static figure. Small jaw. Stop sign. Slowly, carefully drawn. Light pressure on the pencil. Hands barely visible, unassertive. Unstable feet.

Orientation in space

Young children who have not as yet learned the rules of "correct" spatial orientation may draw the human figure upside down or sideways. I have watched children of four and one of five as they drew their figures starting from the feet and working up to the head or drawing the figure as though floating weightlessly in outer space. These few children appeared sociable and alert. They showed no behavior suggesting emotional or developmental disability.

Inversion of the figure is highly unusual even in children. The only explanation that occurs to me in the case of the very young is that it manifests the arbitrariness of many of our rules. The young children who have done it their way may be displaying originality.

The same inversion by older individuals cannot be dismissed so casually. If not deliberate as in Chagall, it suggests difficulty in relating to the environment. It may prove to be a highly significant item in a comprehensive diagnostic procedure.

FIGURE 7

Drawn from feet upwards: feet, tummy, chest, head, hair, eyes, nose, mouth. C.A. and M.A. — 60 months. Tracy has drawn her figure from the feet up, inverting the usual sequence, and printed her name from right to left. She is entering kindergarten with no presenting problems. Drawing and printing were done by her right hand.

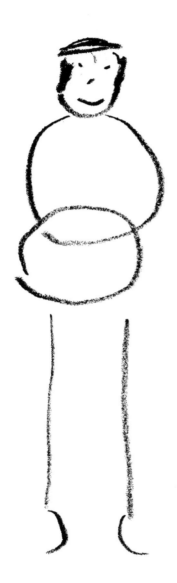

TART

Shading

Another indicator that has received verification in numerous experimental studies is the shading that often obscures the underlying figure totally or in specific parts. This feature is interpreted as an expression of anxiety. It occurs, in fact, in drawings by persons whose anxiety is an outstanding element of their behavior.

Shading that is used with artistic intent, to create an illusion of third dimension, is not to be confused with the telltale type of shading under consideration.

FIGURE 8

By boy, age 4 years 5 months. His home was destroyed by fire.

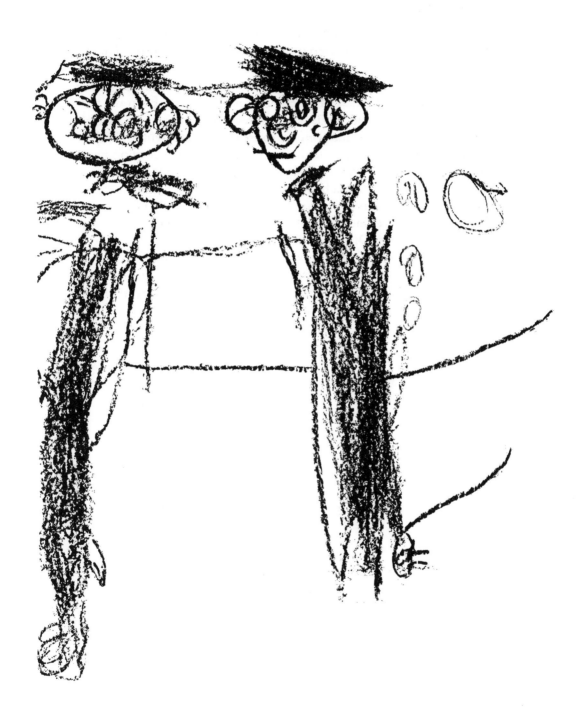

Integration

It is highly unusual for the human figure to be drawn in a disjointed manner with body parts scattered over the page. This finding achieves greater significance when it occurs beyond the preschool years. Typically, the drawing of a person is a unitary figure, an integrated whole from the very beginning, even when far from complete. Even the tadpole figure with arms and legs issuing from the head represents a whole person, whose parts, though few, are those viewed as essentially representing a person at that particular stage in the child's development.

I have seen disjointed figures in drawings by two four-year-olds — one a bright girl, the other a boy. Neither displayed any behavior suggesting emotional disorder (Figures 9 and 10). On the other hand, several children age five and over who drew disjointed figures did show behavioral disorders (Di Leo, 1973).

Failure to integrate the figure is so unusual as to warrant special attention. As a projection of personality disorder, its significance rises with the age of the person. Gradual integration of the figure on followup tends to coincide with clinical improvement.

FIGURE 9

Scatter of body parts. Drawn by Tina, a bright, well-adjusted child, age 3 years 9 months.

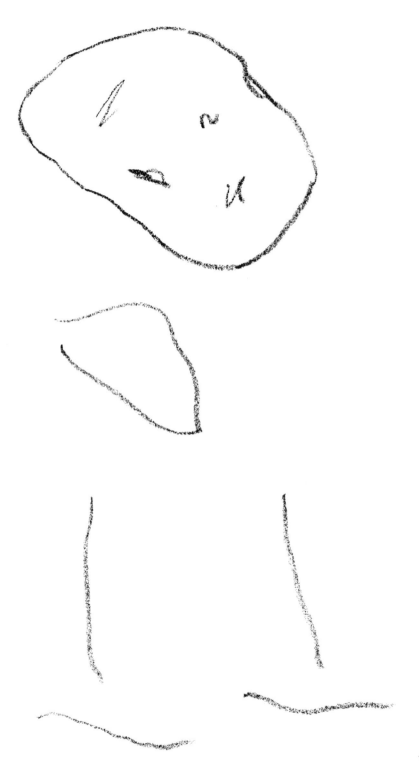

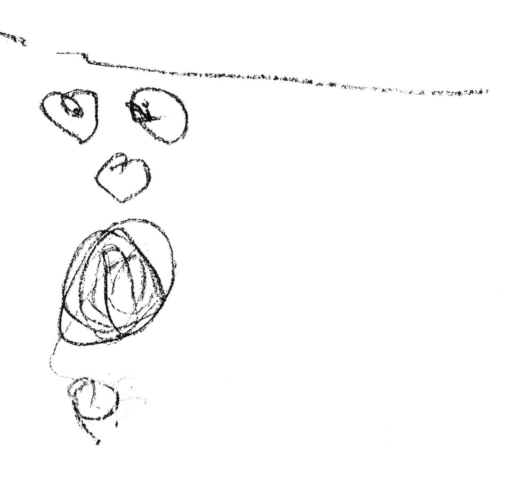

FIGURE 10

By James, age 4 years. Scatter of features.
No outline of head. He named eyes, nose,
body, bow tie. Alert, friendly. Pleasant
disposition. No behavior problem.

Symmetry and balance

In Figure 11 Brenda, age 10 years 7 months, first drew a female figure well to the left of the midline of the page and then balanced it with a male equally well away from the midline to the right. In addition, she constructed each figure symmetrically so that right and left of

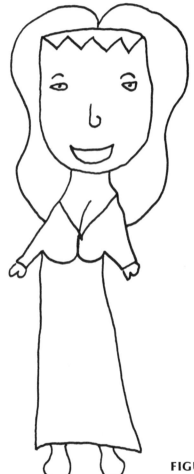
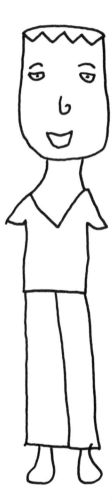

FIGURE 11

By Brenda, age 10 years 7 months.

each is identical (except for the nose). Brenda drew carefully and deliberately, rarely lifting the pencil from the paper. She gave me the impression of having planned the arrangement before beginning to draw and not of improvising as she went along.

The general effect is of rigid immobility. And though the sex of each is clearly conveyed, there is a schematic, stereotyped quality about the figures, which is even more strikingly evident in the drawing of her family that appears in the chapter on Body Parts.

What significance can be attached to symmetry and balance when they assume so prominent a role? Quite simply, they may be attempts to achieve an aesthetic effect, either spontaneously or in deference to adult influence. One may hope that considerations of symmetry and balance shall not block free expression.

Rigid, stereotyped figures occur in drawings by withdrawn adolescents and adults as a projection of defense against what is perceived as a threatening or overwhelming environment.

Extreme preoccupation with symmetry and balance is a feature of Art Brut. The reader is referred to Chapter 12 on Emotional Disorder Reflected in Drawings for a discussion and illustration.

Style

Style may be defined as a manner of expression that is proper to a person or period. It is by the style that a work is attributed to a particular author, composer, or artist, as though it bore an authentic signature. At a glance, one recognizes a work as by Chagall or Matisse. Even in Picasso, who painted in a variety of styles, one can attribute the work to the "blue" or "rose" or "cubist" period and so relate it chronologically.

In child art, individual ways of representing may persist over prolonged periods, thereby permitting a distinction from depiction of the same subject by other children. The emergence of style is contingent on some degree of technical skill such as is not available before school age. Style may be restrained or exuberant, impressionistic or expressionistic, realistic or imaginative. The examination of drawings made at intervals of time may reveal a style that expresses the child's own bent.

Drawing style and quality of line

The insecure infant between the ages of 18 and 24 months approaches a drawing situation hesitantly, touches the crayon cautiously with finger-tips, eventually dares to grasp it and to make a few barely visible, tiny markings in a corner of the paper. Grown older, the insecure child draws the human figure with small, wavering, broken lines, creating a small figure, off center.

In contrast, the secure infant reveals a joie de vivre in a bold, vigorous scribble that is made with strong pressure across the length and breadth of the available space. Later, in drawing the human figure, freedom from stifling anxiety will be expressed in the size of the figure and in the dash and good pressure of a line that tends to be continuous as the figure is positioned in the center of the page and not hidden in a corner.

Even the earliest scribbles can tell us something important about the personality of the child. The descriptions I have given are typical, having been observed by others and by me in literally thousands of children. However, the above clinical observations require qualification when one considers the drawing styles peculiar to talented artists. Picasso tends to outline his figures in an unbroken line that, drawn without apparent effort, bends and twists as it rhythmically encloses the figure giving it substance and vitality. Daumier is more likely to achieve an effect of motion by many short, wavy lines. Here too, the result is impressive, though the technique is quite different.

In my collection of drawings by emotionally disturbed children, there are specimens of both styles: the slow, continuous, unbroken line and the numerous, rapidly drawn—one might say scribbles—were it not for the fact that the drawing is representational despite the over-abundance of apparently irrelevant, redundant circular elaboration.

Just as in adults, artistic talent has often been detected in the work of children who do not conform to generally accepted standards of behavior. It has been stated that during the phase of inspiration that precedes the actual creation of a work of art, the maker is entirely out of contact with reality. In a subsequent chapter, I shall discuss the essential difference between artistic creativity and madness. For the moment, I wish merely to suggest that alienation from the real world, as most perceive it, may be a temporary constituent of artistic expression.

It seems to me that an artist like Picasso, who makes a remarkable line drawing without lifting the writing instrument from the surface, exhibits not only a mastery of form but a concept that is always a step ahead of the obedient hand. Drawing with innumerable short wavy lines may produce an effective result but it gives the impression that the artist is working not from a preconceived theme, but rather in a free, create-as-you-go style. Both are certainly valid, admirable ways of artistic expression.

Drawing is a very personal matter. Each drawing is a reflection of the personality of its individual maker.

3

MOSTLY COGNITION: THE CHILD DRAWS A MAN IN A BOAT

A dichotomy separating cognition and affect is justified as but a device to facilitate presentation of the complex processes under consideration. Such division assumes a duality that does not exist and that is conceivable only where the personality has been seriously disrupted by mental illness.

In devoting separate chapters to drawings viewed as expression of thought and feelings, no compartmentalization is intended; both are aspects of an indivisible entity. An effort must be made to keep sight of the whole while looking at the part — not always an easy task.

Yet, when presented with a relatively neutral stimulus, the response tends to be predominantly cognitive, though not entirely so. And when the stimulus is more personal, the response will tend to mobilize feelings.

With that in mind, I asked one group to draw a man in a boat as a neutral stimulus. Since none of them had been shipwrecked, it was unlikely to evoke an overshadowing emotional response. The other group was asked to draw a house. This was intended as a more personal stimulus likely to evoke a response imbued with affective elements to a greater degree than where the stimulus was relatively neutral.

The following drawing sequences are presented to illustrate the progress of children's thought from kindergarten through second grade, roughly from age 5 through 7. I have selected by way of illustration their rendition of "a man in a boat."

Four stages can be identified along the continuum. In the first, the person is entirely contained within and visible through the hull. What exists must be shown (Figure 12).

In the second phase, the figure begins to emerge. At first, the head, then the upper part of the body appear above deck. But still conforming to the rule that what exists must be shown, the lower part of the body is also visible, though through the hull (Figure 13).

The third phase is an attempt to preserve the integrity of the body while avoiding the illogical transparency. This dilemma is resolved by placing the whole person on deck (Figure 14).

Thus far, the child has been drawing in Piaget's stage of preoperational thought, still viewing the world subjectively and drawing an internal model. The "X-ray technique" is but a reflection of the child's egocentricity.

Only during the fourth phase does visual realism take over from intellectual realism. Now, we see only those parts of the body that are actually visible when a person is in a boat (Figure 15). This phase of visual realism falls within Piaget's stage of concrete operations and is usually achieved between 7 and 8 years of age.

Figures 12, 13, 14, 15a, and 15 are by contemporary American children. In 1887, there appeared in Bologna the first book in which actual children's drawings were reproduced. The author was neither professional psychologist, educator, nor pediatrician, but a famous art critic fascinated by child art and gifted with brilliant intuitive and perceptive qualities. In his book are progressive renditions of the theme "man in a boat." One will see the identical four phases as in the drawings by children today (Di Leo, 1970).

A century and four thousand miles separate us from Corrado Ricci's children but the mental processes implicit in solving the problem of how to draw a man in a boat continue to be identical.

Drawings and cognitive development

Representational drawing begins sometime between 3 and 4 years with the chance discovery that what had been mere scribbling can now be made deliberately to symbolize something in the visual world. This something is likely to be a person represented by a head. Soon, two smaller circles will be the eyes and another the mouth. It will

FIGURE 12

By boy, age 5 years 5 months. Phase I:
Person within the hull.

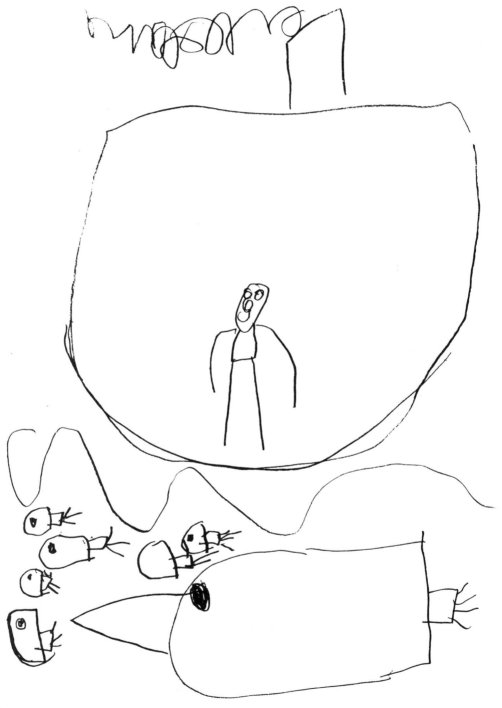

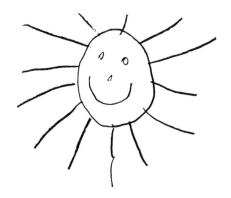

FIGURE 13

By boy, age 5 years 7 months. Phase II:
The person begins to emerge.

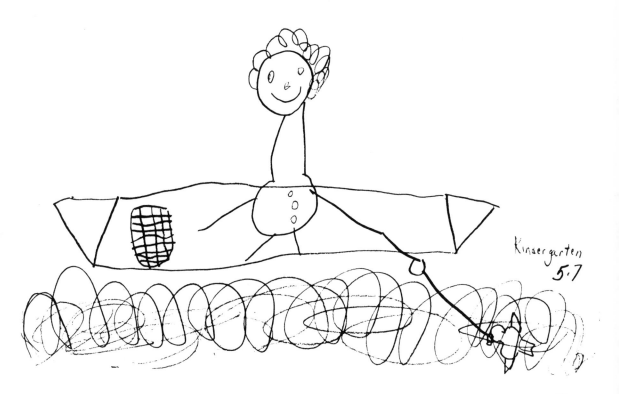

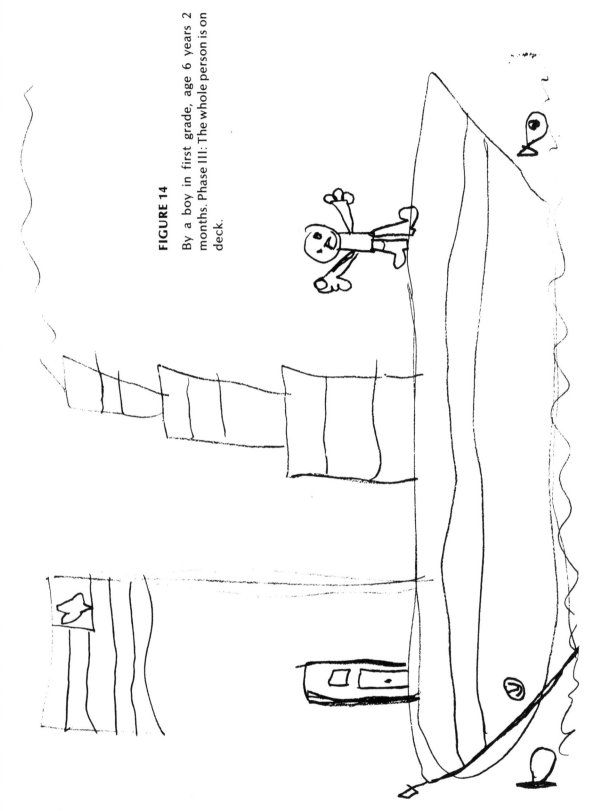

FIGURE 14

By a boy in first grade, age 6 years 2 months. Phase III: The whole person is on deck.

FIGURE 15a

By a boy, age 6 years 6 months, in first grade. Phase III–IV transitional: He has shown only the part of the body that is actually visible when a person is in a boat. He has not, however, shown the same logic in this treatment of the face, which is clearly visible through the beard.

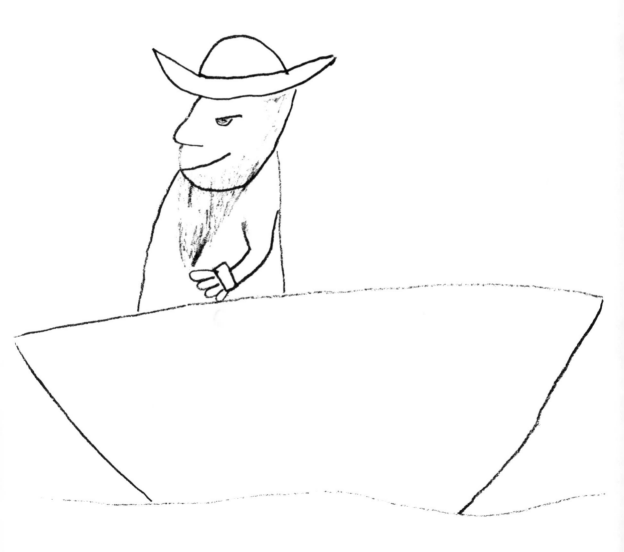

FIGURE 15

By a boy, age 7 years 7 months, in second grade. Phase IV: Visual realism is evident in this drawing. No part of the person is visible through the hull; nor is any part of the trunk visible through the arms. There are no transparencies. The partly submerged oar is correctly portrayed.

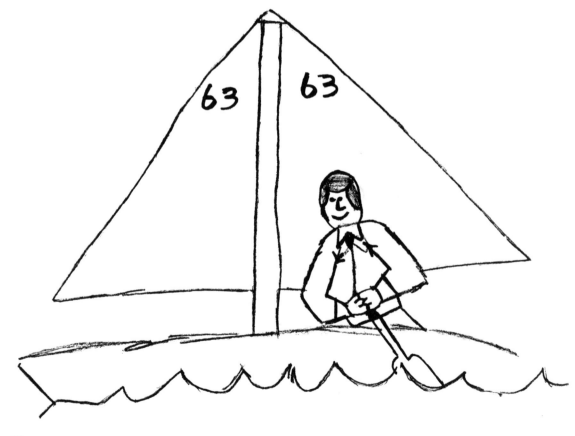

not be long before lines will issue from the huge head and we shall have the essentials of a person reduced to tadpole form. This first representation of the human form has been observed wherever children's drawings have been studied, now as in the past.

It is not surprising, since nothing is so vitally important to the child as people. The human figure shall remain the child's favorite subject. This preference has been confirmed by numerous investigators (Di Leo, 1970; Goodenough, 1926; Harris, 1963; Luquet, 1913; Maitland, 1895; Ricci, 1887).

During the preschool years, spontaneous drawings tend to be more elaborate with the inclusion of other items of significance, notably houses, trees, sun, and other aspects of nature. Uniformity of sequences in drawing behavior, though not in time of their appearance, reflects the orderly progress of cognitive development. Human figures in particular are regarded as valuable indicators of cognitive growth and are the basis for measurement in the Goodenough and Harris procedures.

A qualitative as well as a quantitative change occurs at about seven or eight years when "intellectual realism" gives way to "visual realism" (Luquet), a change that finds its correspondence in the Piagetian concept of a shift from the preconceptual to the concrete operational stage. These terms express, in substance, a metamorphosis in thinking from egocentricity to an increasingly objective view of the world.

Though cognitive development will manifest its progress also in house and tree drawings, these do not lend themselves to the same degree of standardization as human figure drawings. They are of limited value as measures of intellectual maturity. More broadly, however, house drawings do document the passage from an egocentric to an objective view.

At earlier (preconceptual) levels of thought, there will be transparencies, such as people visible through walls, simultaneous view of three sides of a house, total disregard of visual perspective, and bird's-eye and frontal view in the same drawing. All these "errors" will gradually vanish as visual realism takes over. Then the child will attempt to draw things as seen by the external rather than by the mind's eye. Distant objects will be drawn smaller, chimneys that were oblique because perpendicular to the slant of the roof will be made vertical, X-ray technique will be abandoned as illogical, and people will no longer be seen through walls.

In brief, the house drawing, too, will reflect the level of intellectual growth but not so sensitively as the drawing of a person. Goodenough/Harris's D-A-P test remains the most reliable indicator of intellectual maturity among drawing procedures.

Development of drawing related to Piaget's stages of cognitive development — A synoptic view

Approx-imate Age	Drawing	Cognition
0–1	*Reflex response* to visual stimuli. Crayon is brought to mouth; the infant does not draw.	*Sensorimotor stage* Infant acts reflexly. Thinks motorically.
1–2	At 13 months, the first scribble appears: a zig-zag. Infant watches movement leaving its marks on a surface. Kinesthetic drawing.	Movement gradually becomes goal-directed as cortical control is gradually established.
2–4	Circles appear and gradually predominate. Circles then become discrete. In a casually drawn circle, the child envisages an object. A first graphic symbol has been made, usually between 3 and 4 years.	The child begins to function symbolically. Language and other forms of symbolic communication play a major role. The child's view is highly egocentric. Make-believe play.
4–7	*Intellectual realism* Draws an internal model, not what is actually seen. Draws what is known to be there. Shows people through walls and through hulls of ships. Transparencies. Expressionistic. Subjective.	*Preoperational stage* (intuitive phase) Egocentric. Views the world subjectively. Vivid imagination. Fantasy. Curiosity. Creativity. Focuses on only one trait at a time. Functions intuitively, not logically.
7–12	*Visual realism* Subjectivity diminishes. Draws what is actually visible. No more X-ray technique (transparencies). Human figures are more realistic, proportioned. Colors are more conventional. Distinguishes right from left side of the figure drawn.	*Concrete operations stage* Thinks logically about things. No longer dominated by immediate perceptions. Concept of reversibility: things that were the same remain the same though their appearance may have changed.
12 +	With the development of the critical faculty, most lose interest in drawing. The gifted tend to persevere.	*Formal operations stage* Views his products critically. Able to consider hypotheses. Can think about ideas, not only about concrete aspects of a situation.

Though the response to a relatively neutral situation may be predominantly cognitive, it cannot be isolated from affective elements. The person is unaware, at least during childhood, that the idea is imbued with unconsciously expressed symbols in its graphic expression — hence, the artificiality of separating out parts from what is in reality a whole with interacting aspects. In writing, as in speaking, one is limited by the inability to present the whole simultaneously. Only the visual arts can offer the whole at once.

The nautical theme as a symbolization of birth

The child's drawing of a person in a boat undergoes changes and becomes more realistic as the child matures intellectually. I believe this to be evident from the examples and discussion thus far.

I should now like to suggest that the theme may be viewed from another aspect. We may assume — and not without abundant evidence — that the child is also expressing unconscious content in the apparently neutral theme of a person in a boat. Apart from their manifest content, the sequences in the drawings suggest a symbolic representation of the birth process. The ship symbolically represents the feminine sexual cavity. Water is related to intrauterine life and birth.

In the drawings that have been presented, the person is first seen entirely within the ship. Gradually, as the sequences progress, the person emerges. At first the head and upper trunk appear, then the rest of the body until the whole person is on deck. These sequences are especially meaningful because they occur during the preoperational years, while the child is still very much an individual, before the culture and intellect impose a logical realistic portrayal.

Bender (1981) notes that seriously troubled children draw boats as symbols of mother within whose body (the hull) they seek security and contentment. The sun often appears in these drawings and symbolizes the father.

4

MOSTLY AFFECT: THE CHILD DRAWS A HOUSE

Affect expressed in house drawings

> "Le dessin d'un enfant c'est
> un peu de son âme. . . ."
> Edouard Claparède

This aphorism of the distinguished educational psychologist is especially applicable when the child is free to choose subject matter and mode of portrayal. What meaning may one derive from drawings made without direction from another person and from sheer personal delight or need?

In drawing a picture, the child seems to project a desire or, perhaps, an attempt to possess the object; if not actually having it, at least having an image of it. Early man painted animals. Lovers treasure a likeness of the loved one. Claude Lévi-Strauss writes that art is based on the illusion of being able not only to communicate with the being, but also to possess it through the medium of the image (Charbonnier,

1969). This view would account for the frequently noted fact that inner-city children often draw country-style houses rather than the buildings they actually live in and see constantly. Also, this would explain why children without a home of their own, living in shelters which they hope will be temporary, will draw the yearned-for home, symbol of the warmth and affection that have eluded them and that only family life can provide.

Drawing to please themselves, children portray people, houses, trees, grass, the sun. These themes are to be seen in the work of children from all lands and cultures, and attest to the basic universality of mind and feelings. The young child tends to ignore or to transform reality into a subjective world rich in fantasy. The drawings are a representation, not a reproduction.

In *Spring Snow,* Yukio Mishima remarks that without imagination, there is no choice but to form our view on the reality that surrounds us.

A house appears frequently in spontaneous drawings

In the assessment of personality, the House-Tree-Person Test (Buck, 1948) is a commonly used projective technique. The subject is simply requested to draw the three in the order named, reserving the drawing of a person to the last, since it is more likely than the others to arouse conscious associations. The selection of the three is based on their assumed symbolic meaning. The house is interpreted as representing the subject's environment, the tree as growth, and the person as an expression of integration of the personality. Apart from considerations of validity of the projective device, it is noteworthy that the three topics are frequently and spontaneously included in children's drawings (Figure 16).

Children regard persons, houses, and trees as significant influences in their lives. In drawing them, they are unaware that they are telling more about themselves than about what they have drawn.

Figure 17 by 5-year-old Maurizio, who attends kindergarten in Rome, is a pleasant scene showing a house with its chimney emitting an abundance of smoke (an expression of warmth and affection within); a tree with broad trunk (dominant emotional life typical of children); and a child with a balloon. The person, though a child, is drawn relatively larger than the house and tree because a person is more significant.

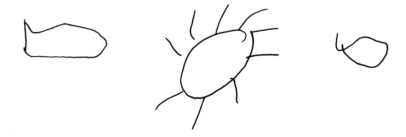

FIGURE 16

Cheryl, age 7 years 4 months, has spontaneously drawn house, tree, person. Large trunk typically seen.

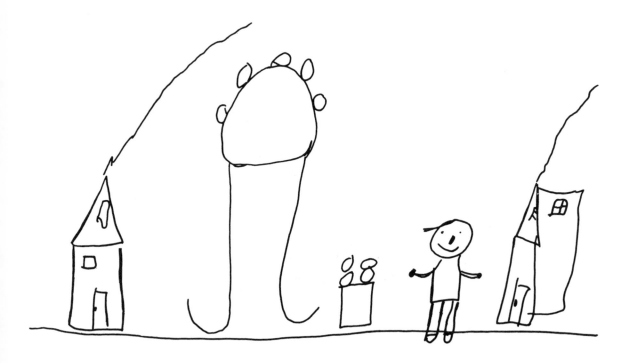

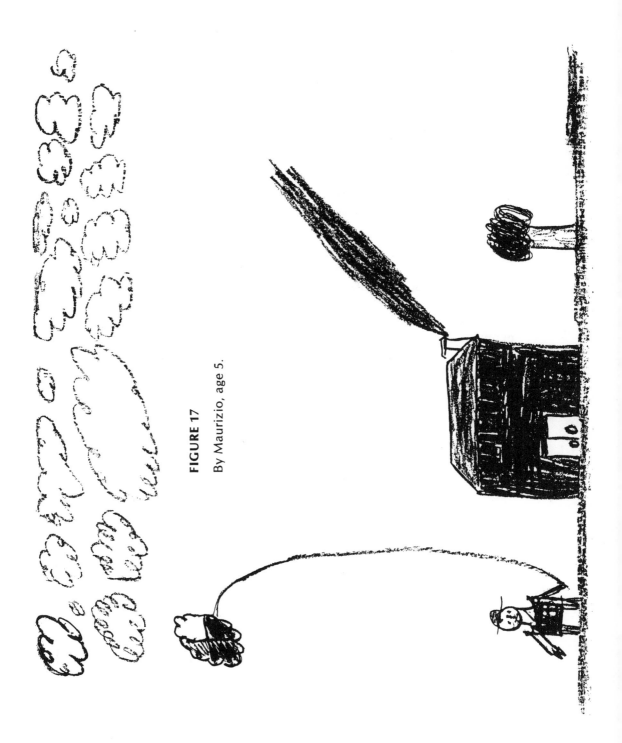

FIGURE 17

By Maurizio, age 5.

Figure 18 by 10-year-old Roberta, who attends fourth grade, is also a spontaneous drawing. She has depicted a girl (herself) jumping rope. Barely a wisp of smoke issues from the chimney and there is a large scar on the tree trunk (symbolizing a traumatic event in her life?). She is in foster care because of a seriously disruptive family situation.

These drawings are among numerous specimens that illustrate the preeminent station that the three entities assume in a child's mental and emotional life.

Diminishing frequency of the house in spontaneous drawings by preadolescents

Houses, animals, and aspects of nature figure prominently, next to the human figure, in drawings by school-age children.

The choice of subject matter expresses the child's interests and needs. The house symbolizes the place wherein is sought affection and security, basic needs that find fulfillment in family life. Animals are often added as part of the family. Trees, flowers, and the sun appear as expressions of a growing need for light, nature, and the world beyond the confines of home. In my study of house drawings by city children, the overwhelming majority drew houses such as are typical of country living—houses with slanting roof and chimney rather than the beehive apartment complex in which most of them actually lived.

An investigation conducted by Morino Abbele (1970) of drawings by Florentine children in grades one through five revealed interesting trends. She found that between the ages of 6 and 7 a house appeared in 60 percent of spontaneous drawings, while aspects of nature were

FIGURE 18

By Roberta, age 10.

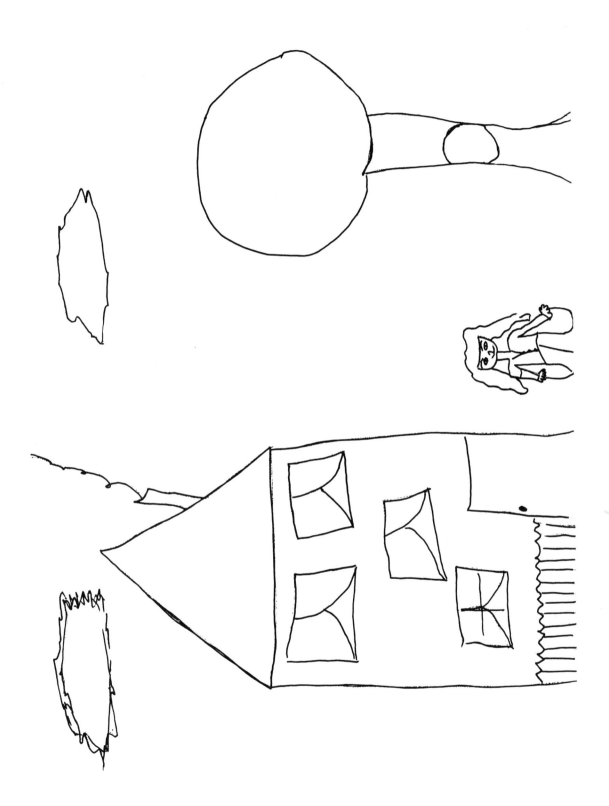

seen only occasionally. But, significantly, as children matured, the house began to decrease in frequency, so that by age 10 to 11 most drawings depicted a scene in which houses might appear only as an item in a broader composition that included trees, flowers, sun, and often the ubiquitous Italian sea. This gradual shift is interpreted as expressing a gradual emancipation from the dominant familial ties of earlier years, as the need arises to enlarge the circle of interests and relationships beyond home and family.

Cognitive features in children's drawings of houses

The broad division between preconceptual and logical thought, between subjectivity and objectivity, between egocentricity and altruism, and, in chronological terms, between below seven and above seven years is manifested graphically by the earlier attempts to represent and the later attempts to reproduce.

Roughly below seven, the child draws what is known to be there regardless of how or if it is actually visible. This inner reality will gradually give way to a more prosaic outer reality devoid of fantasy. The passage from subjectivity to objectivity is not abrupt; both ways of "seeing" may coexist well beyond age seven.

Typically, children will draw the chimney at a right angle to the plane of the roof. If it is a slanting roof, the chimney will be on the bias. It will be some time before the chimney will be drawn vertically regardless of the inclination of the roof. This correction expresses an advance in the level of thinking; it is dependent upon a mental operation that is not as yet available to the child who draws the diagonally oriented chimney.

FIGURE 19

By Judith, age 7. The house is in frontal view, but swimming pool and path are in bird's-eye view. As known, not as actually visible.

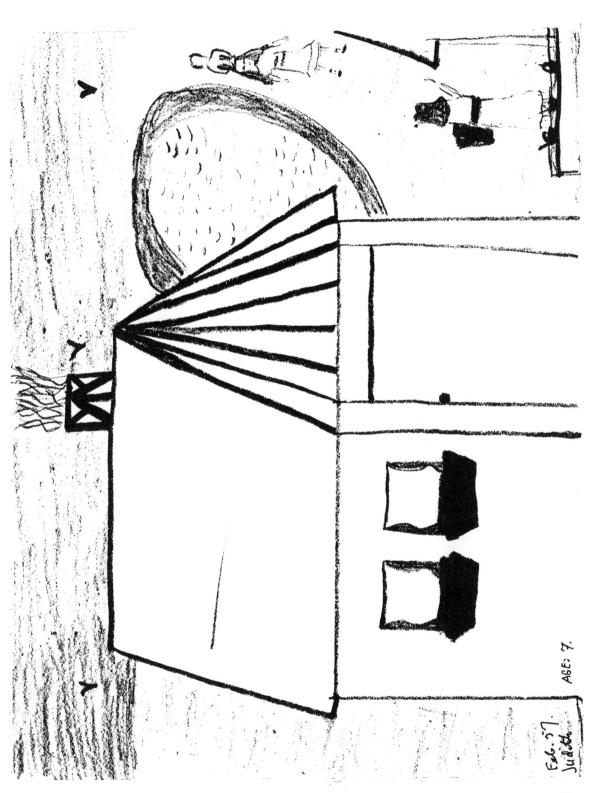

Feb. '67
Judith

AGE: 7.

47

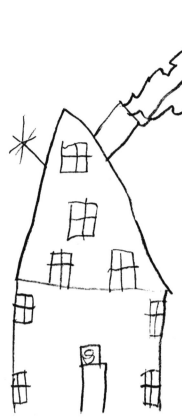

FIGURE 20

By Jerry, age 8. The chimney and antenna are perpendicular to the slant of the roof. That is how most children his age and even older will draw the chimney.

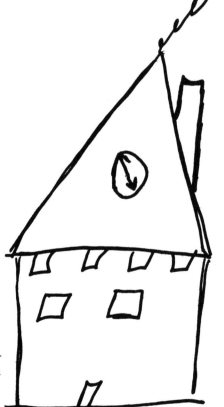

FIGURE 21

Chris, age 11, has drawn the chimney upright, showing that he has surmounted a significant cognitive hurdle.

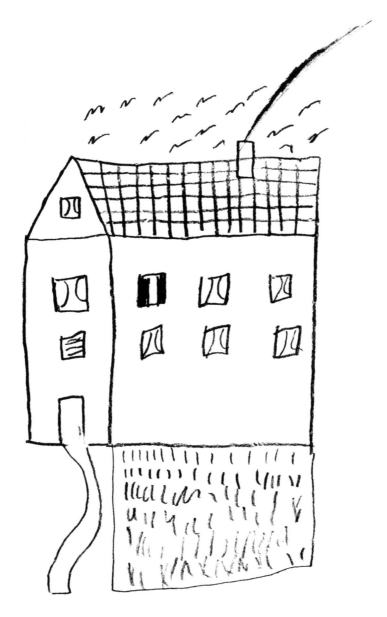

FIGURE 22

By Alfred, age 11, shows a house in frontal view with path and lawn in bird's-eye view. As known, not as actually seen.

But while the preceding drawings may be viewed dispassionately for their cognitive elements, this one (Figure 23) by Alfred conveys an overall impression of melancholy that overshadows its intellectual attributes. The boy has drawn the distant buildings smaller than the car in the foreground revealing a major step forward in perceptual development: the notion of perspective.

It is interesting to note that placement of the more distant objects on a higher plane is similar to the device employed by Chinese artists during the thirteenth through the eighteenth centuries. Linear perspective in art appeared in the Western world during the early Renaissance.

More striking in this drawing is the cemetery with its three crosses. His home was disrupted. His parents are separated and he is awaiting placement with surrogate parents. I believe the three crosses to symbolize the three persons who constitute his family. They are lost as though dead.

FIGURE 23

Alfred, age 11 years 5 months.

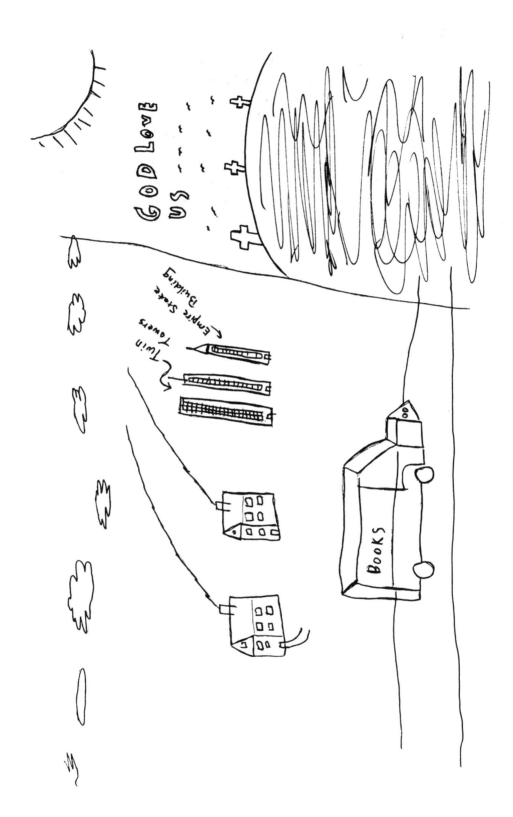

GOD LOVE US

Twin Towers

Empire State Building

Books

The house as a haven

Figure 24 is drawn by a boy of 12. He is living in a residential treatment center, because his parents have separated and gone their own ways with no provision for parental care. A nurse has taken him for a weekend visit to her home. His typical belligerency gave way to peace and contentment during the visit. Slowly and meticulously, he has drawn this cross-section of her home.

I believe that he has drawn what has impressed him and what he is yearning for. The light bulb in the living room symbolizes warmth. There is a TV and lamp in the bedroom, four place settings in the dinette, and a neat bathroom.

FIGURE 24

FIGURE 24

By Francis, age 12.

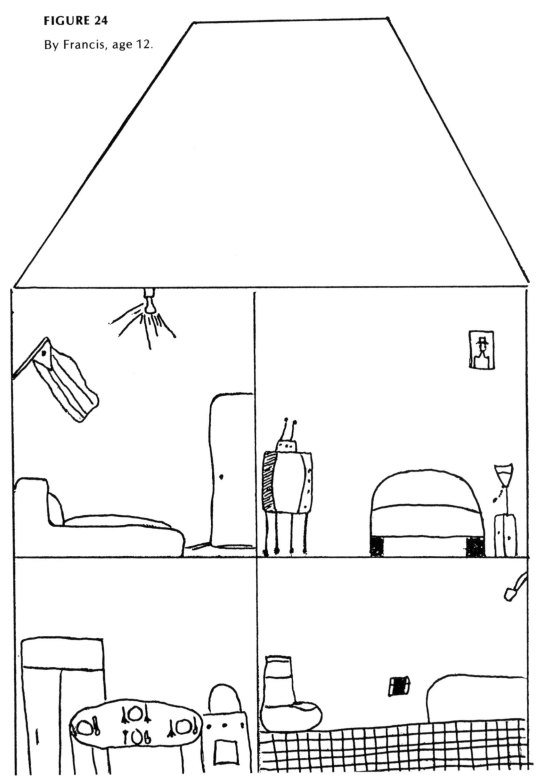

Figure 25 is drawn by a girl of 9. The apartment is enlivened by the presence of family members in the bedroom. Toys, pictures, and flowers as well as the usual TV are outstanding features of pleasant connotation, while furniture has been omitted except for a bed and stove. Everything for play, rest, and food to keep them smiling.

FIGURE 25

By Clara, age 9.

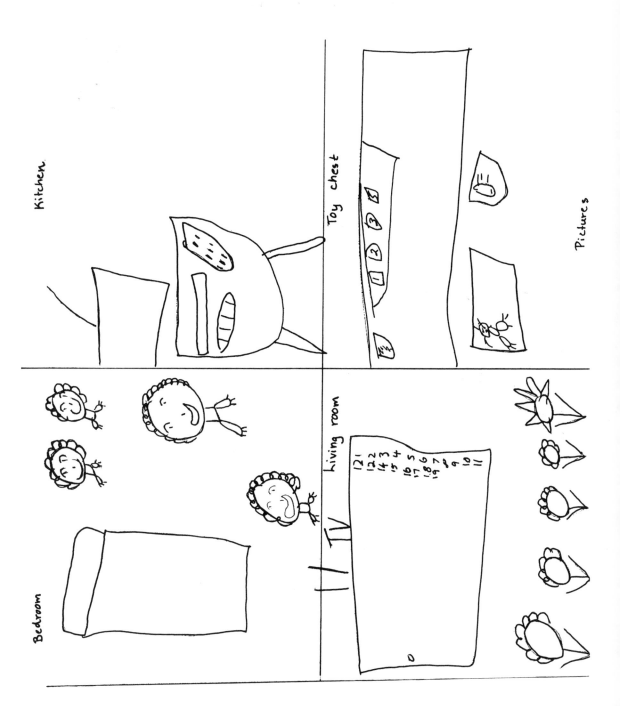

Kitchen

Toy chest

Pictures

Bedroom

Living room

Figure 26 is drawn by Sean who has endowed his house with facial features. It is not just an inanimate object.

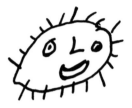

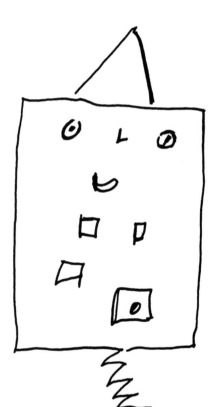

FIGURE 26

Anthropomorphized house by Sean, age 10.

In Figure 27 a television set is shown, as in almost every drawing that depicts the inside of a house.

When requested to draw a house, children will invariably draw the exterior. A specific request to draw the inside must be made if one is to obtain an interior view.

If the house is perceived as a home with all its connotations of warmth, protection, security, and love, children may vitalize it with the significant people in their lives.

The house as a female symbol

In discussing the symbolism of dreams, S. Freud (1949) attributes female symbolism to the house and its rooms as representing the womb, while doors represent the genital opening. In interpreting children's drawings, I have found little value in this approach, since almost anything that has a capacity to contain or to get in and out of has the same allegedly symbolic meaning (boats, cars, jars, bottles, pockets, etc.).

Despite the confusing ubiquity of sexual symbols, the association of womb and haven is undeniable. Unconscious feelings may be rising to the surface as the child consciously draws a house.

Implications for architects

What inferences may be made from the drawings, assuming—with reason—that the children are expressing unconsciously their wishes and needs?

The clear preference for the small country-style house in a setting of trees and flowers, brightened by a smiling sun, should be taken into account when planning housing for families. The needs of all children for light and air and safety will more properly be met in a two-story garden apartment dwelling than in the beehive-type high-rise structure in which thousands of city children actually live. They are deprived of contact with nature and exposed to hazards of contact with strangers in elevators and stairways, and the sky is seen through window guards that are rendered necessary for safety.

Just as architects are sensitive to the needs of the handicapped, it is gratifying to know that the needs of children are now being given serious attention.

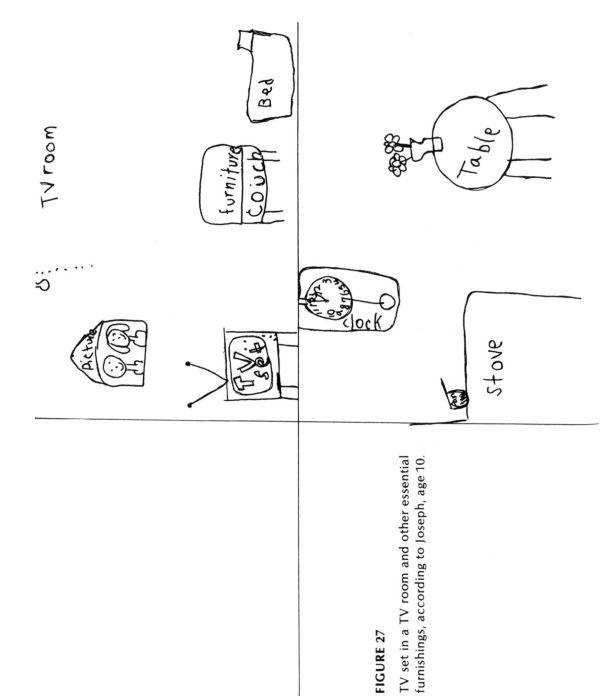

FIGURE 27

TV set in a TV room and other essential
furnishings, according to Joseph, age 10.

5

THE PROJECTIVE SIGNIFICANCE
OF CHILD ART

Drawings viewed as projections
of personality

It is generally recognized that children's drawings, especially those of the human figure, express the child's level of intellectual maturity. The scoring of these drawings has been carefully developed and standardized by Goodenough (1926) and to a greater degree by Harris (1963, 1970), and strongly positive correlations have been found with the Stanford-Binet and Wechsler Intelligence Scale for Children (see Harris, 1963, for a summary of correlations). The scoring is basically quantitative and analytical, with points attributed to details and, to a lesser degree, to basic structure.

Long, widespread use of the test has confirmed the original contention of Goodenough and Harris that the method is of universal application and that it is a reliable and valid measure of the cognitive abilities of young and preadolescent children.

The same acceptance has not been conceded the drawings when

they are viewed as expressions of the unconscious projection of the emotional aspect of the personality. Their use as a projective technique has failed to satisfy the standards required of a test. The analytical approach has yielded generally poor correlations. As a result, the drawings have met the fate of other projectives in being viewed with skepticism by the more scientifically oriented investigators. The subjective element in interpreting the drawings introduces a practically uncontrollable variable (Di Leo, 1973).

And yet, despite lack of experimental support, clinicians continue to value drawings as a means of establishing rapport and as expressions of personality traits and perceptive abilities (Winnicott, 1971). A voluminous literature attests to the interest aroused by the art of children as expression of thought and feelings. Thus far, assessment and interpretation of feelings have eluded measurement by the methods currently available.

It is my conviction that each drawing is a reflection of the personality of its maker; that it expresses affective aspects of the personality as well as cognition; that it is telling, in the case of young children, more about the artist than about the object portrayed; that the approach of the examiner must of necessity be intuitive as well as analytical.

Having conceded that the drawing is telling something, I believe that the message will become more apparent when the product is viewed as a whole. Unfortunately, despite admonitions by Machover (1949) and others that the drawings be viewed holistically as well as analytically, excessive emphasis has been placed on the search for specific symbols of archetypal and psychoanalytic significance. This has often led to a point-by-point mechanistic procedure (see Chapter 6).

Projective techniques cannot meet the reliability and validity standards of psychometric tests. Nevertheless, they remain valuable tools in the hand of the experienced clinician. Those who have become familiar with their use will not do without them, as they search for clues that standardized tests are unable to supply.

Expression of emotion in child art

Great artists and sculptors have stirred emotional response in the viewer in a variety of ways: by color, bodily attitudes, scene, as well as by facial expression. Endowed with deep insight into human nature, uncommonly keen powers of observation and perception, and the technical skill to express these gifts in visual form, the masters communicate life and feelings. Titian, Velasquez, Rembrandt, Bernini, and Van Gogh, among others, have created works that astonish the viewer as greater than life. Such mastery is far beyond the abilities of even the most gifted children.

Apart from an unconscious expression of feelings and attitudes which may imbue their drawings and paintings, children may give deliberate expression, but this is limited to facial expression.

In my experience, young children are too immature to explicitly express any but the most obvious states of feeling in their drawings. At best, they can convey directly feelings of joy and sorrow, hostility and fear. I suspect that the expressive features in many of the specimens in my collection have been influenced by characters in comic strips. It is only at adolescence that we may reliably expect more subtle emotional states to be represented consciously.

The drawings that follow are some of the attempts by children to give expression to their characters. In Figures 28 and 29, James, age 11, has drawn a male figure expressing contrasting moods. This he has achieved by appropriate orientation of mouth and eyes. There may be some connection with the fact that James was brought to professional attention because he was high-strung, enuretic, and emotionally labile. His nails were bitten down.

FIGURE 28

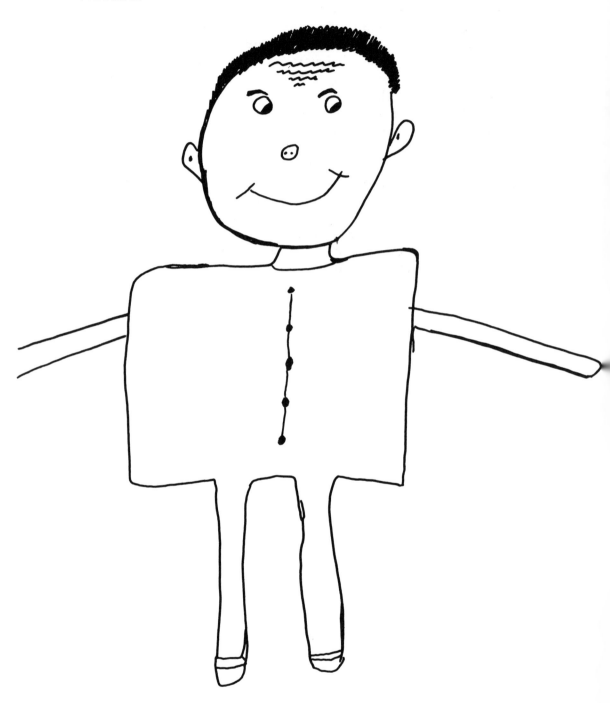

FIGURE 29

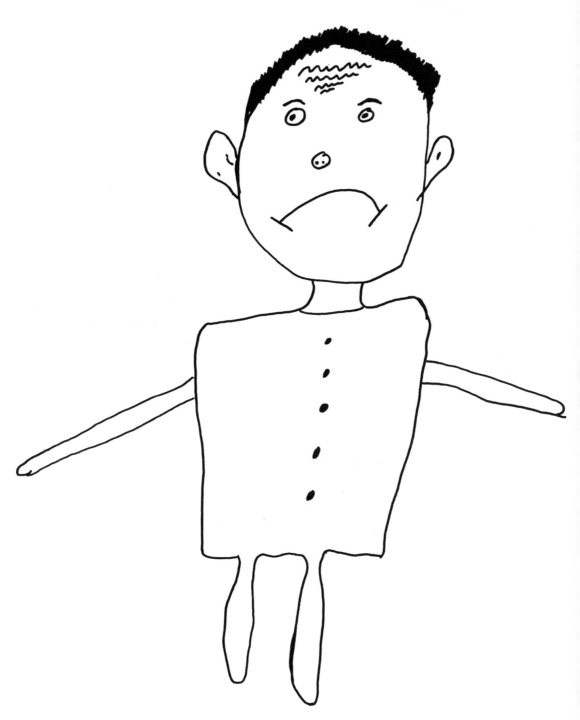

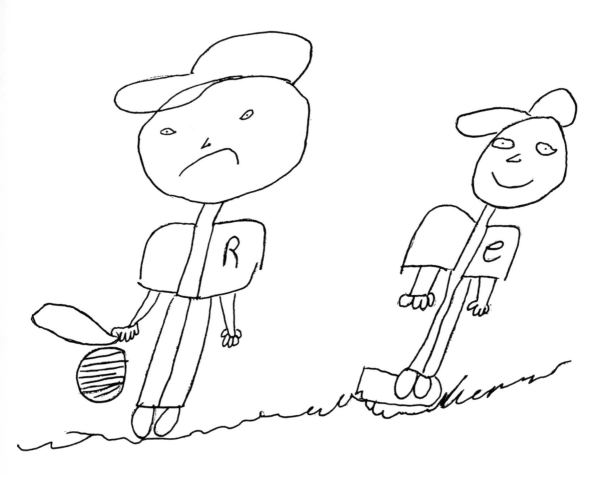

FIGURE 30

Drawn by Anita, age 10 years 2 months. Two ball-players. "The first one is mad because he missed the ball. The other one is happy because he hit a home run."

Minimalism and stereotypy

Minimalistic, stereotyped projection of the body image is noted in drawings by insecure, depressed children and in those by regressed psychotic adults.

A child's poor body image is reflected in Figure 31 drawn by a girl of 7 years whose father has abandoned the family but who is nevertheless very much in her thoughts. She has drawn him first. Of good intelligence, she has just been promoted to second grade.

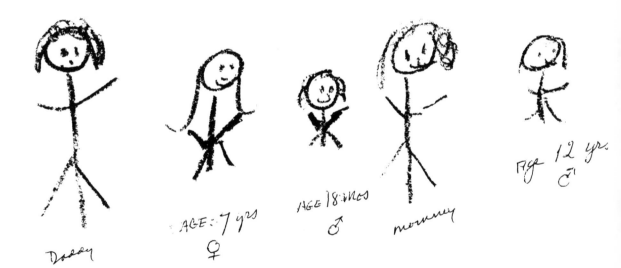

FIGURE 31

Family by Clara, age 7. Though father is no longer living with them, she has drawn him first. Mother is near the end, beside the older brother drawn last and smaller than herself.

Figure 32 is by a boy of 6 years. He has been transferred to a residential treatment center because of abuse in his home.

In Figures 32 and 33, the human figures are stereotyped and impoverished. I have observed similar treatment of the human figure in an extensive collection of drawings that I have studied, made by children from broken homes and requiring their temporary transfer to a group home pending placement with surrogate parents or possibly back in their own, reconstituted home.

Minimalistic treatment of the human figure by regressed adults is described and illustrated in Arieti's *Creativity: The Magic Synthesis* (1976).

Personal space as a function of trust and self-esteem

Personal space as a buffer between child and unfamiliar adult is manifest during the third trimester of the child's first year. The 8-month-old infant typically hugs the parent when approached by a stranger. Piaget has dealt with space as a cognitive development, tracing its progressions through maturing concepts of distance, depth, and perspective.

Along with this growing awareness of spatial relationships, there is a social aspect in which the child's need for space seems to function as a protective device, whose amplitude is inversely related to the degree of trust and positive feelings experienced in the presence of another person. Closeness to the parent contrasts with distance from the stranger.

Studies have shown that the need for space between peers becomes manifest only at about age five. Prior to that time, children associate more freely with others of the same age.

As the child approaches school age, the need for distance in peer relationships has been correlated with the child's self-image and sense of trust. The child's self-esteem is decisively influenced by the interaction between the child's intrinsic forces and the attitudes and behavior of the significant persons who constitute the child's world. Evidence of self-esteem may be observed in human figure drawings. Insecure children tend to draw a small person in contrast to the large, boldly-drawn figure typical of secure children (Di Leo, 1970, 1973).

Stratton, Tekippe and Flick (1973) in a study of college students of both sexes found that those with a high self-concept approached others more closely than those with low self-concept scores on the Tennessee Self-Concept Test. As expected, Sommer (1969) and Horowitz, Lewis and Luca (1973) found that schizophrenics chose more distant seats from other persons.

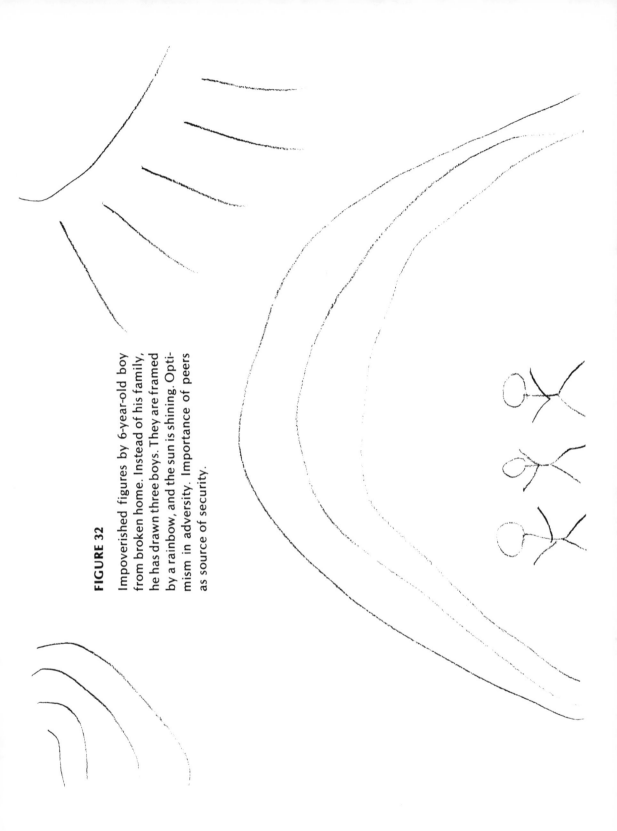

FIGURE 32

Impoverished figures by 6-year-old boy from broken home. Instead of his family, he has drawn three boys. They are framed by a rainbow, and the sun is shining. Optimism in adversity. Importance of peers as source of security.

FIGURE 33

In this drawing of his family, Raul, age 7 years 6 months, from a broken home, has drawn himself away from his parents, closer to his dogs.

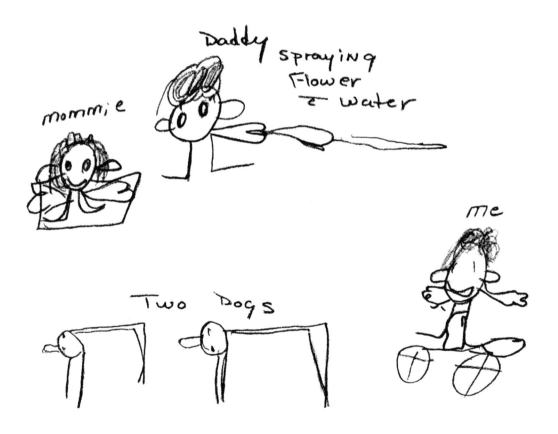

mommie

Daddy spraying Flower ᵴ water

me

Two Dogs

Correlation between personal space and human figure drawing

Bonino, Fonzi, and Saglione (1978) devised a methodology for measuring the variations in personal space as determined by the distance that an individual child selected when asked to sit with an unfamiliar child of the same age. The subjects were 11-year-old boys. A bench was provided, long enough to offer ample space between the two boys; its back was calibrated so that the intervening distance could be measured. From among 200, 30 were selected as showing clear differences: 15 chose to sit close to the stranger, while 15 kept a "safe" distance from the other.

The 30 children were then asked to draw a person. An interesting, significant correlation emerged when the two results were compared: The size of the human figure was noted to be inversely related to the buffer distance assumed by the two groups. Those who sat near the stranger drew larger human figures in contrast to the smaller figures drawn by the boys who sat farther away from the other boy.

The need for greater buffer space and the smaller human figure drawing were interpreted as indicators of insecurity and lower self-confidence.

Cognitive-affective ratio: see-saw effect

If we compare the human figure drawn in response to the request "draw a person" with that to "draw your family," it will be noted that the lone figure is often superior qualitatively as well as quantitatively to the figure drawn as part of the family group. This disparity has suggested to me that there is a see-saw effect in the cognitive-affective ratio to account for the superiority of the product that results when the child is simply asked to draw a person, since such a request tends to elicit a predominantly intellectual response: The child draws what is known and remembered. On the other hand, a request to draw the family is likely to elicit a response imbued with affective elements resulting in less concentration on what is known and more on what may be felt vis-à-vis the other family members.

In naming this the cognitive-affective ratio (Di Leo, 1973), I have recommended that the lone human figure be used for evaluation by the Goodenough-Harris test of intellectual maturity and not a figure extracted from the family group.

Figures 34 and 35 illustrate the difference, when one compares the father as a lone figure with the father in the family drawing. The lone figure has ears, neck, insertion of the arms at the shoulders, pockets, correct number of fingers among parts that are lacking in the father in the family group.

FIGURE 34

Father, drawn by A. G., age 11 years 3
months.

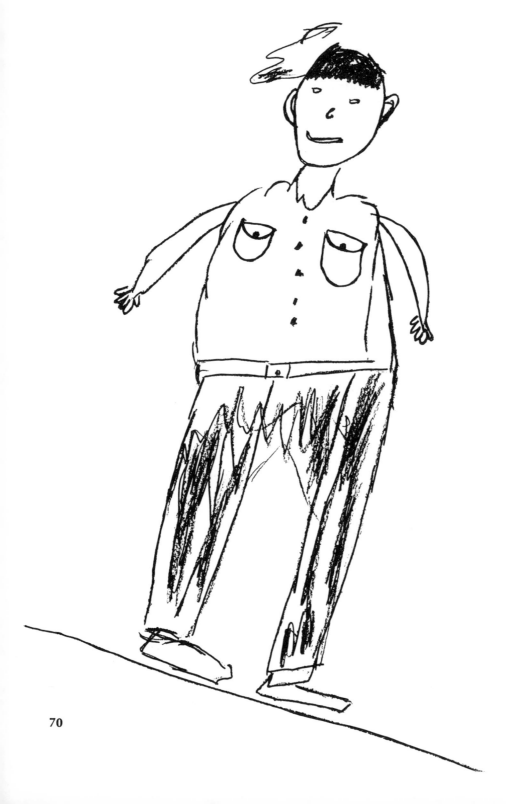

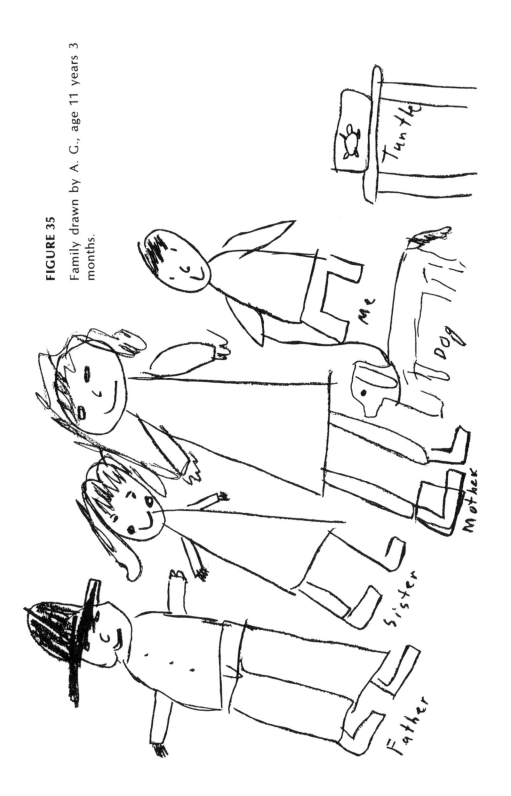

FIGURE 35

Family drawn by A. G., age 11 years 3 months.

Family drawings: feelings and interpersonal relationships

Beyond manifest expressions, there are features of the drawing style and content that are symbolic of the child's feelings and attitudes. These features may be expressed unconsciously by the child in drawing the family group. Their interpretation is a challenge to the clinician who believes that the surface structure is but a cover to the greater reality that lies beneath.

Omission of Self from the group is often seen in drawings by children who feel rejected. This omission has been seen by me in too many drawings by adopted children during adolescence, when the concern over identity raises the inevitable questions, "Who am I?" and "Who are my real parents?"

Compartmentalization is a term used to indicate separation of one member from another by surrounding each with a frame, so that each is boxed in. This expresses lack of communication and feelings of isolation (Figure 36). Feelings of isolation may also be expressed by distance, by the need for psychological space, as when the child separates self from parents by an intervening piece of furniture or TV set.

The mother cooking or serving food symbolizes the dispenser of warmth and love. Depiction of mother engaged in vacuuming or cleaning is interpreted as symbolic of prime interest in order. The domineering parent is likely to be drawn larger than the other, regardless of actual physical dimensions.

FIGURE 36

Encapsulation, by Armando, age 13. From: *Il Complesso di Laio* by T. Giani Gallino. Einaudi Editore.

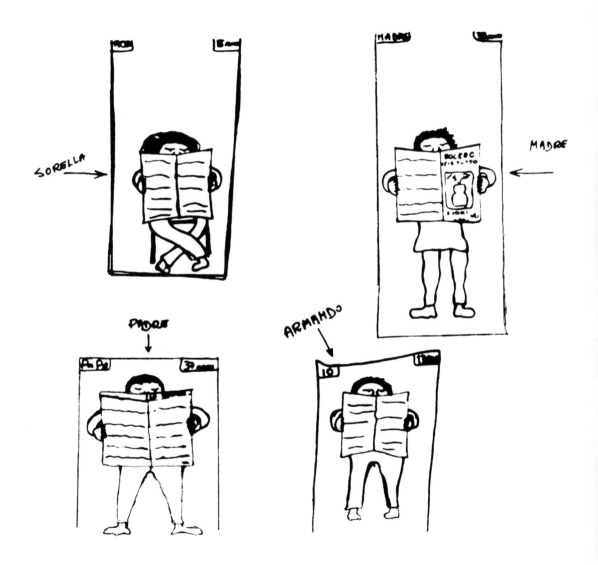

Father watching TV, smoking, eating by himself, or hiding his face behind the newspaper suggests withdrawal from the family's concerns or activities (Figure 37). Placement of the subject near or away from a parent or sibling indicates preference or negative feeling.

Resistance to drawing the family has been noted in children whose home life is characterized by turmoil and violence, and who have acquired an intensely negative image of family.

Family drawings as vehicle for the expression of feelings

The Kinetic Family Drawing (K-F-D) (Burns and Kaufman, 1970, 1972) is a valuable projective technique for exploring family interplay. It should be obtained after a family drawing made in response to a request that the child draw the family. This is important because without this prior drawing a golden opportunity will have been lost to see whether the child would have included the Self within the family group. Once this drawing has been obtained, the K-F-D should follow with the specific instruction to include Self.

To exploit the drawing situation fully, the order of presentation should be:

1) draw a person (indicates sex drawn first)
2) draw the other sex
3) draw your family (has Self been included? who has been omitted?)
4) draw your family including yourself, everybody doing something (interplay among family members).

FIGURE 37

By Lisa, age 11. While mother and daughter are busy at household tasks, father is complaining that he can't ever read the newspaper in peace. From: *Il Complesso di Laio* by T. Giani Gallino. Einaudi Editore.

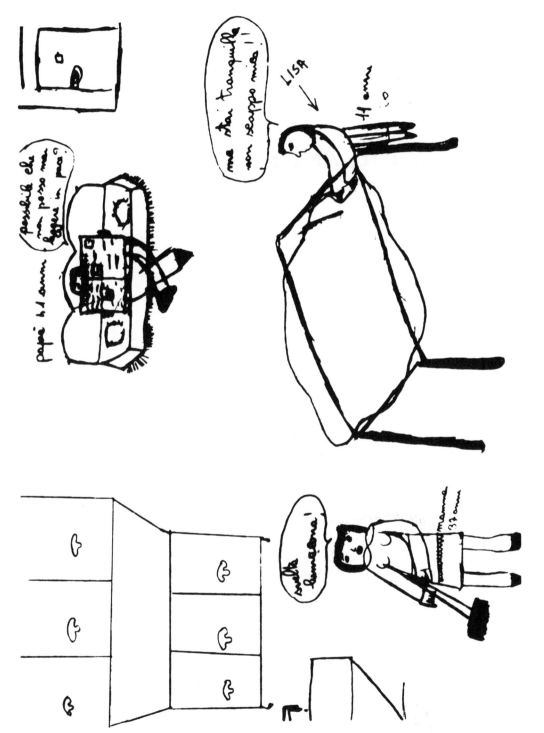

6

THE WHOLE AND ITS PARTS

In her pioneering study, Machover (1949) presented a method for interpretation of human figure drawings. Assuming the drawings to be projections of the body image, the author identified numerous specific indicators. Within the framework of psychoanalytic theory, meaning was ascribed to the manner in which parts of the body were emphasized or omitted. But despite Machover's caution that structural and formal aspects of the drawing were as meaningful as content, the attention directed at details of the figure tended to obscure the vision of the whole, giving rise to checklists of traits from which a point-by-point interpretation might be derived. In many instances, the significance attributed to specific indicators failed to withstand the test of experimental verification (Swenson, 1968).

In his classical work on human figure drawings as expressions of cognitive development, Harris (1963), though willing to recognize that they undoubtedly contained projective features, considered them to have low validity as measures of affect and personality.

Undeterred, clinicians continue to value drawings of a person (D-A-P) and of the family (D-A-F and K-F-D) as revealing expressions of personality, despite the incredulity of those who concede existence only to that which can be measured. The intuitive approach to intangibles (self-image, feelings, conflicts, relationships) resists quantification. A global approach eludes measurement of its inherent subjective element.

Atomism and holism

Atomism, a term derived from the physical sciences, has been borrowed by the behavioral sciences to indicate the action of individual parts.

The term *holism* is widely used by natural as well as behavioral scientists to express the view that an integrated whole is more than the sum of its parts. The term has an unusual etymology, owing its origin not to a psychologist, philosopher, or scientist, but instead to Jan Christian Smuts, a South African general (1870–1950). He saw the determining factors in evolution to be whole organisms and not their constituent parts. The concept extended to the behavioral sciences accounts for the primacy accorded the whole in evaluating behavior and its products.

Details

Relying solely on specific details may be misleading. The overall impression is generally a more valid indicator. In my experience, details have greater symbolic meaning when they appear in drawings by adolescents and adults.

In Figure 38 the absence of hands might be regarded as lack of confidence in social contacts or passivity. The stick legs and unstable footing could suggest insecurity, while the darkened cloud might symbolize an obscure threat in the offing. These negative features, however, contrast with the impression of joy conveyed when the drawing is viewed globally. The sun is shining on a happy girl with her balloon. She is flanked by tulips. Sun, girl, and balloon have happy faces. The artist, a well-adjusted girl of 8, has many friends. The scholastic year has just ended and she has been promoted to third grade. The family is intact and well functioning. (Incidentally, sun and balloon are on what is projectively regarded as the male [father] side.) The global impression is in tune with her behavior.

Conflicting indicators impede interpretation and render significance of the drawing obscure. Interpretation should be deferred. Follow-up drawings are desirable if available without alarming the family.

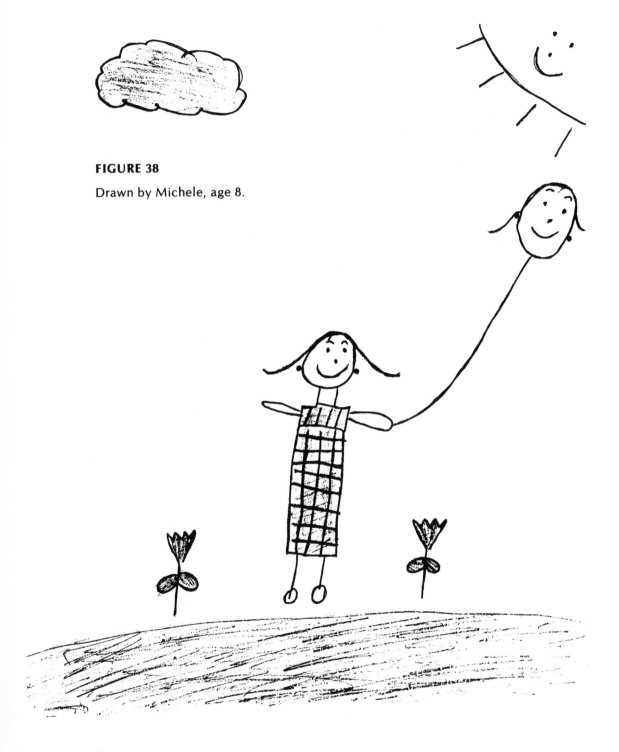

FIGURE 38

Drawn by Michele, age 8.

Figure 39 is a spontaneously drawn scene by Tina, age 10. She is a child of Hispanic parents. She speaks Spanish and, with some difficulty, English.

The overall impression is of a little girl picking flowers in a garden setting, flanked by a house and a tree. The chimney is smoking (warmth within) and the sun is shining from the upper left (maternal side). But there are "ominous" details, namely: large clouds, one of them darkly bordered; a tree closed at the crown (self-contained); shaded trunk (anxiety); dark scar (trauma); base-line (support); herself as small as the flowers (self-image). The overall impression may be pleasant, but hardly serene.

The child is in fourth grade because of her problem with the English language. There is no known traumatic event in her clinical history to account for the black knothole; nor does she manifest behavior that is unusual in girls her age. She lives with her family and appears well-adjusted. There is no presenting problem. This drawing should be kept for possible comparison with her future drawings.

FIGURE 39

Conflicting indicators in a drawing by Tina, age 10.

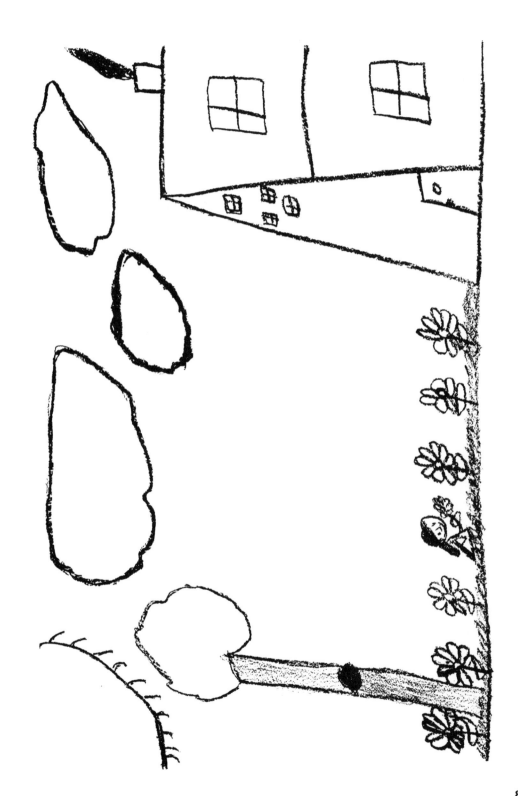

Drawings are but a part of a comprehensive assessment. They are aids in diagnosis and therapy.

A holistic approach to drawings is not intended as neglect of the significance of individual items. These call for special attention when there are many pointing in the same direction. How many items are required for validity is not so much a matter of number as of quality.

There is a hierarchy of signs. Some are clearly more unusual and significant than others, such as the explicit portrayal of genitalia. In Figure 40 the impressive penis and huge muscles can hardly be ignored as representing aggression in the 11-year-old boy who said that that's what he wants to be like. Other items—ears, trunk—do not speak so blatantly.

FIGURE 40

Drawn by a boy of 11 years showing how
he wants to be when he grows up. Machis-
mo.

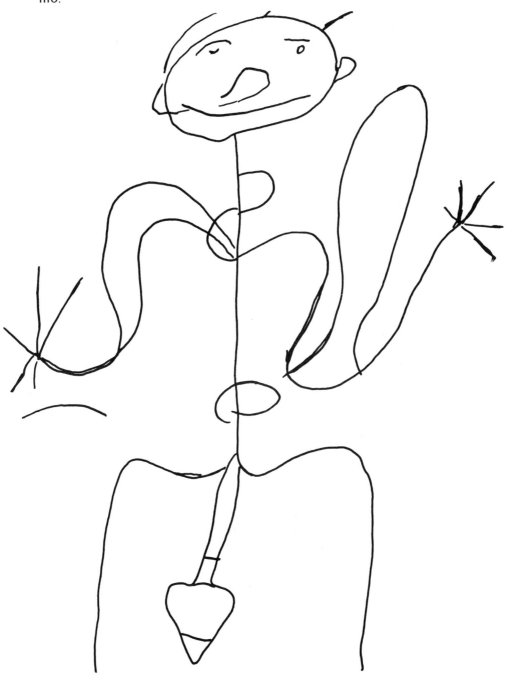

In Figure 41 a child of 5 years 6 months has drawn her mother and herself. The figures are tiny, insignificant. She is living alone with her mother, father having deserted the home. The child is bright and quite articulate. When I asked her to draw her family, she said, "But I have only two people in my family, me and mommie." The figures are unstable, lacking feet, and they are tiny. The general impression derived from the drawing suggests insecurity—an impression that concords with the reality of the situation in the home.

In evaluating drawings, one feels more comfortable when there is a cluster of items in accord with the impression conveyed by the whole.

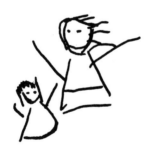

FIGURE 41

Drawn by a girl of 5 years 6 months. Her father deserted. She has drawn mother and self: tiny, unstable figures.

Hard and soft sciences

In the interpretation of drawings, the question of validity remains unresolved. The human sciences cannot provide the degree of objectivity that is attainable in the physical sciences. The complexity, variability, and unpredictability of human behavior preclude the certainty expected in simpler, physical phenomena. Extreme examples of the hard and soft sciences are offered by Stent (1980) as he contrasts the objectivity in mechanics with the ambiguity in psychoanalysis.

We are reminded by Aldous Huxley (1977) that the one desire of scientists is to have a standard to work upon, but that the human being is "very, very far from standardized" and that it would be indeed surprising if the great physical and physiological differences in people did not influence their behavior.

And nothing has been said of the variable that is the viewer. Even the most experienced and skillful cannot escape the effect of influences that have fashioned thought, feelings, and a personal approach to the human material under investigation.

These are sobering but not discouraging thoughts, for ours is not an all-or-nothing situation.

Parts attain meaning within the global context

I believe that a first global view of drawings should precede and thereby lay out a context for evaluation of individual parts.

Parts are significant in relation to each other and to the whole. The individual part affects the whole and reciprocally achieves its measure of significance within the context of the whole. A parallel may be drawn with what occurs in the human body when one part is diseased or damaged: the body is affected globally. But the degree to which the body is impaired is determined by the body as a totally functioning organism. The last word resides in the whole.

Our knowledge of persons is not mathematical. It does not depend upon the enumeration of component parts. It originates from a general impression of the whole, which like a mythological Oriental god has many faces, not all visible at one time. The impression is influenced by both viewed and viewer.

7

GLOBAL FEATURES

Size

Paul, age 4, was walking with his mother in Central Park when his attention was suddenly attracted to a lone pedestrian coming towards them. Concerned, Paul turned to his mother and said, "Mommy, isn't he afraid to be walking alone without his Mommy?" The object of concern was an adult dwarf.

Well beyond the preschool years, children will draw large figures to indicate their importance, in complete disregard of their actual dimensions.

The illusion of movement

"Movement is life."
Leonardo da Vinci

Among the devices used by artists to create the illusion of movement are the *sfumato* or blurred image, anticipatory tension in the viewer, and the use of rapid, energetic strokes.

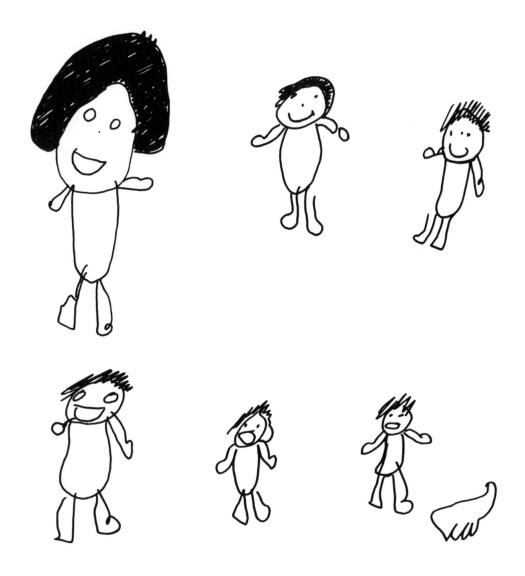

FIGURE 42

Drawn by a boy of 7 years 6 months. Size expresses the child's perception of the relative importance of family members. He has excluded himself.

FIGURE 43

By boy, age 9.

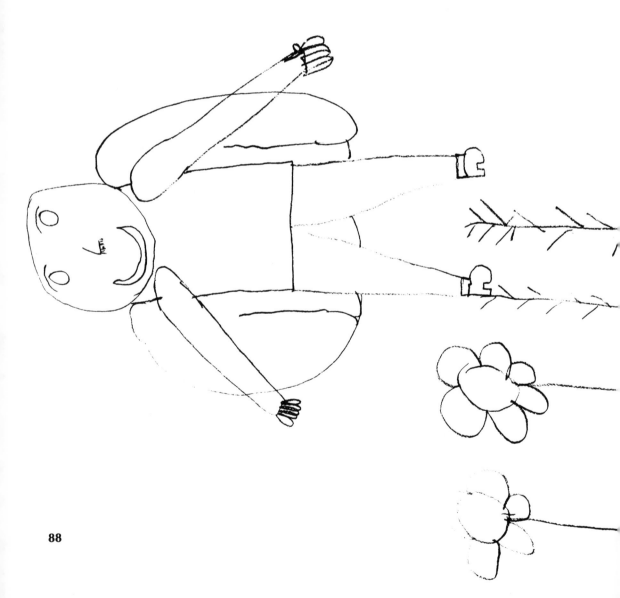

The blurred image perfected by Leonardo da Vinci conveys the illusion by stimulating the viewer to sharpen the image. Anticipatory tension is created by stimulating the viewer to mentally complete the action. The rapid sketch is more effective in conveying the illusion of movement than is the detailed polished style. Compare the vitality of Guardi's Venetian scenes to the stately but static renditions of the same by Canaletto.

The only way we know something is alive is because it moves by its own power. Spontaneously or imitatively, children use a variety of devices in their desire to impart movement to their figures. Generally speaking, boys are more likely to portray action, while girls seem to be more interested in detail and finish.

The depiction of movement

Children of school age, no longer satisfied with their full-face static figures, attempt to depict them in movement, hoping to create an illusion of movement without motion. Realizing the difficulty of indicating movement in a full-face drawing, they discover the profile orientation as offering a more effective orientation for depicting walking, running, and doing.

Various devices are employed; some of them obviously imitative of those used by comic-strip artists. Yolanda, age 11 years 8 months, has succeeded in conveying the illusion of movement by showing her father with the heavy dumbbell over his head. The huge biceps muscles help the viewer perceive the drawing as a static moment in a continuing action (Figure 44).

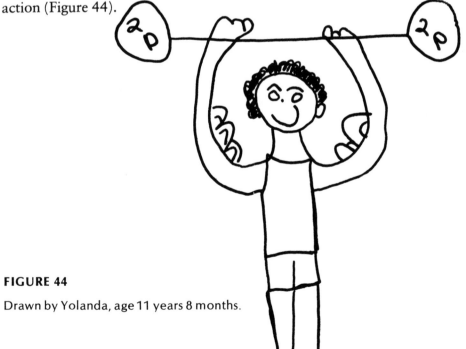

FIGURE 44

Drawn by Yolanda, age 11 years 8 months.

In Figure 45 James, age 12, by orienting his figure in profile, has clearly shown him to be fishing. This action would be extremely difficult to portray in a full-face drawing.

FIGURE 45

Drawn by James, age 12.

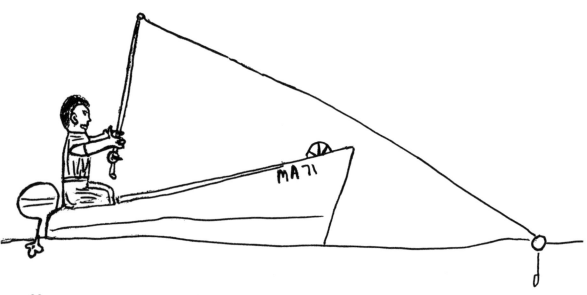

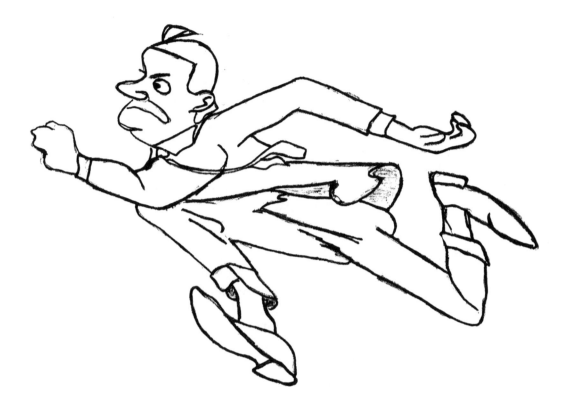

FIGURE 46

By Marty, age 12. Good except for the runner's right arm.

Sex drawn first

Numerous studies have confirmed the generally accepted view that the vast majority of children draw their own sex first when requested to draw a person. It has also been observed that the percentage of girls drawing their own sex first declines with the approach of adolescence.

These findings have been related to sex role. The change that occurs in a significant number of females does not represent, in my opinion, a shift in role or sexual identification, but rather an expression of interest in the other sex. The female is about two years ahead of the male in attaining puberty.

It will be interesting to see whether changes in sex drawn first will reflect the social and cultural changes that are obliterating the role models that have prevailed in the past. But stereotypes die hard. The child's conservatism in portraying the human figure is slow to give way.

Figure 47 was drawn by a female of 18 years. She is a cosmetician who is living at home in an intact family and is described as well adjusted. Like many adolescents, she had to be prodded to draw. After protesting that she did not know how to draw, she acquiesced. The shoulders of the youth are broad, the hips narrow. There are erasures of the trouser legs and of the right arm and hand. The attention to hair suggests the influence of her occupation.

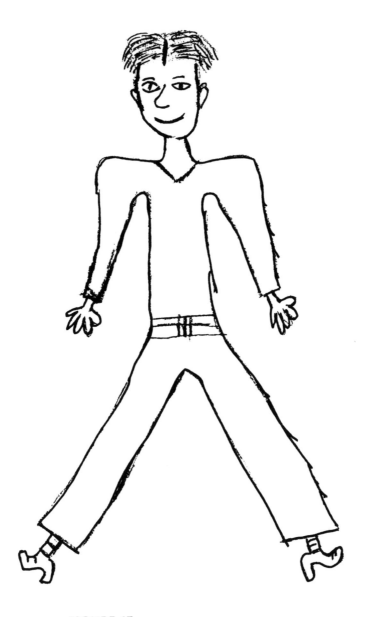

FIGURE 47

Requested to draw a person, an 18-year-old female has drawn a male first.

Omission of self from the family group

This occurs in drawings by children who do not feel themselves appreciated. The omission may be deliberate or an unconscious "forgetting."

In my experience this has occurred with greater frequency in adopted children as they approach adolescence, the time when identity becomes a major concern, even among those living with their natural parents.

For that reason, I have insisted on obtaining a family drawing by simply saying "draw your family," before requesting a kinetic-family-drawing (in which the child is to draw the family including self) and thereby wasting an opportunity to determine whether the child would have included self spontaneously in the family group.

Figure 48, by Grace, age 8 years 3 months, was drawn in response to a request that she draw her family. She has omitted herself. When she indicated that the drawing was completed, her absence from the group was pointed out to her, to which she replied, "I don't want to draw myself—I don't know what I look like." Grace is living in her own home with her natural parents and siblings. She is jealous of her brother. There is a clinical picture in which psychosomatic vomiting and bragging bravado are prominent features. Inferiority feelings and sibling rivalry are reflected in the omission of herself from the family as represented. There is no problem at school. She is in third grade and doing well.

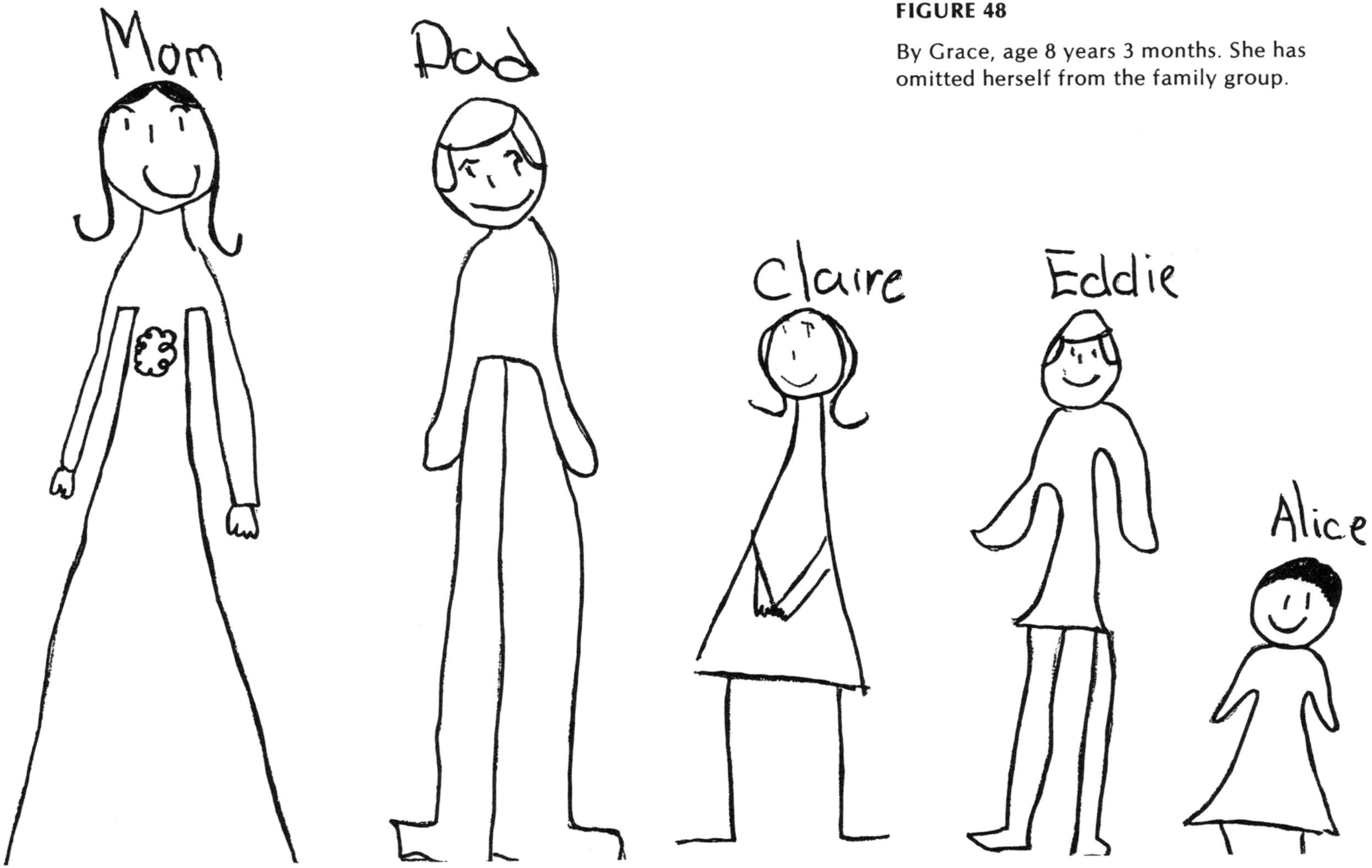

FIGURE 48

By Grace, age 8 years 3 months. She has omitted herself from the family group.

The absent mother

In Figure 49 Bobby, a bright 5-year-old attending kindergarten, has drawn his family. Though his mother is physically absent and he is being cared for by his paternal grandfather and his father, he has included her in the group—a denial of an unacceptable reality. His mother does not visit. Bobby says that his father is interested only in beer (Oedipal level of development).

FIGURE 49

By Bobby, age 5.

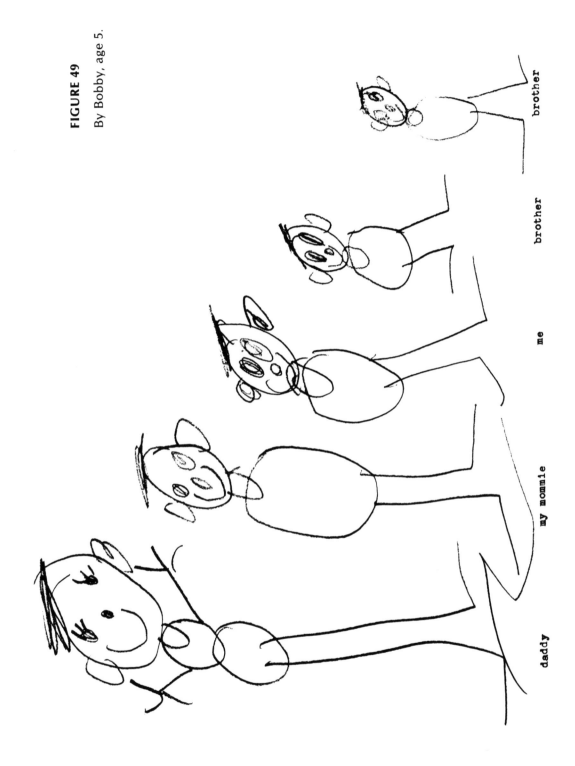

brother

brother

me

my mommie

daddy

Figure 50 is by Tina, age 11 years. She has excluded her mother from the family group and depicted herself and father engaged in household activity (late prepuberty phase of development).

By including his absent mother, the 5-year-old expresses attachment despite her neglect. By excluding her mother, the 11-year-old girl expresses resentment while accepting the fact, as she busies herself with what has to be done in the home.

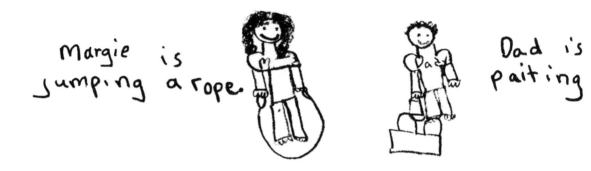

Margie is jumping a rope.

Dad is paiting

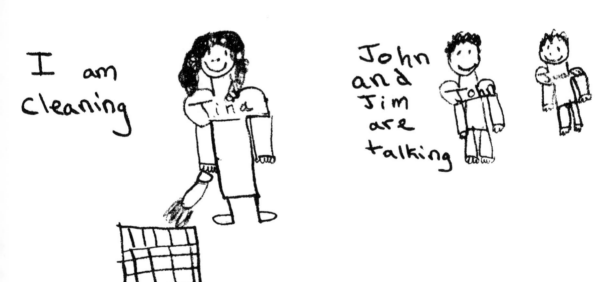

I am cleaning

Tina

John and Jim are talking

FIGURE 50

Drawn by girl, age 10 years 11 months. Broken home—mother absent from family group.

The absent father

This is more commonly the situation than that in which the mother is absent. Usually the effects are less profound.

Figure 51, drawn by a girl of 9, eloquently portrays father as more of an apparition than a reality.

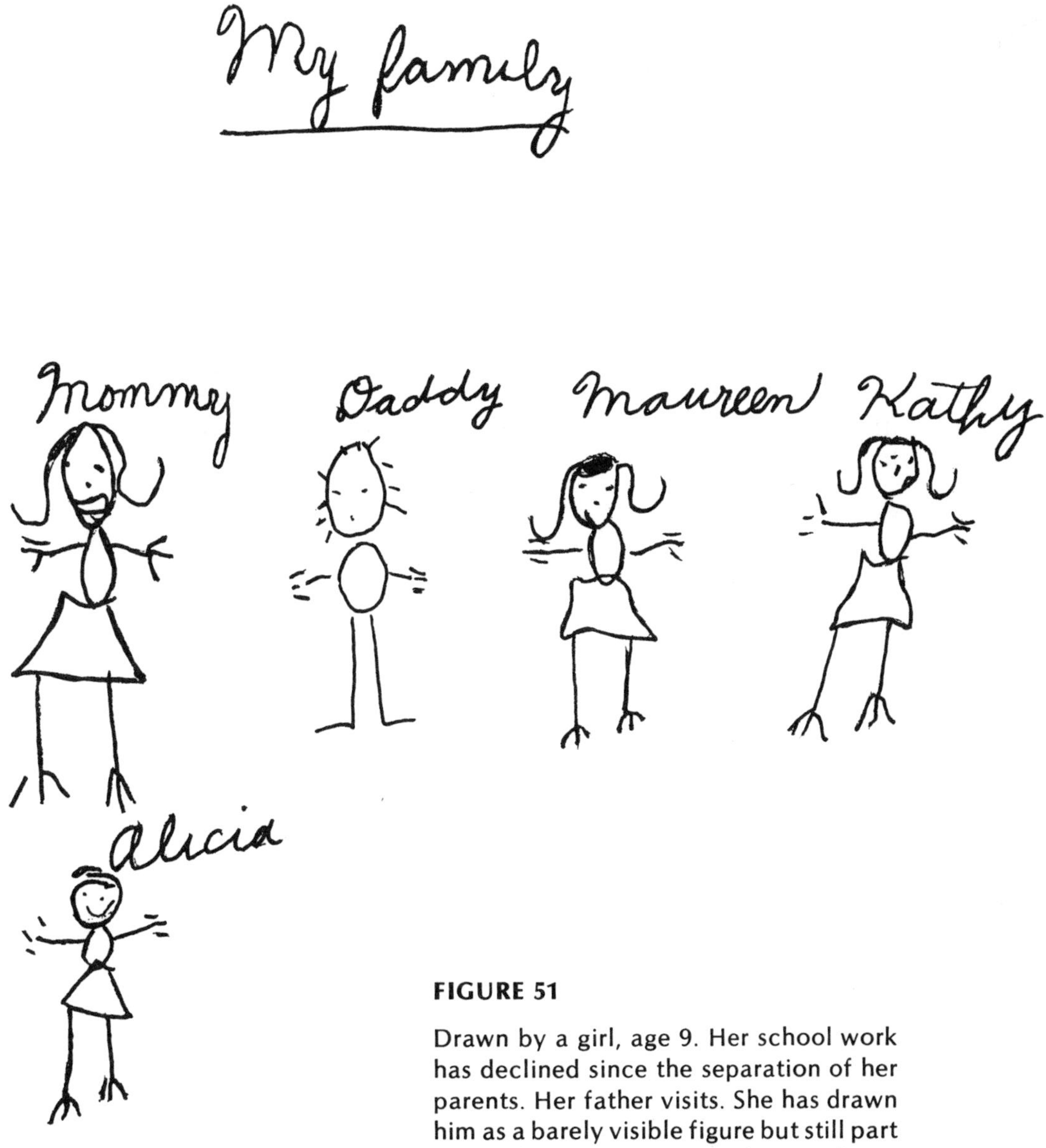

FIGURE 51

Drawn by a girl, age 9. Her school work has declined since the separation of her parents. Her father visits. She has drawn him as a barely visible figure but still part of her family group. He's there and he's not there.

Figure 52, by a girl of 10, shows mother watching television and Gloria herself with her cat and dog.

The father does not, however, fulfill his role merely by being present. He must also be available physically and functionally. The father who comes home from his office, is greeted by his dutiful wife with cocktail in hand, removes his shoes, and buries himself in the newspaper is hardly devoting loving attention to his family. It is quite revealing to see how many children, when asked to draw their family, will make father hiding his face behind the newspaper, deliberately removed from the activity and cares of family life. There are limits to how much one should give to the job. Then again, there are those men whose leisure hours are dedicated to playing golf or tennis or watching sports on TV. Children have drawn their fathers doing those things apart from their children who justifiably feel neglected and emotionally isolated from the parent they need as a role model.

A more obviously deplorable paternal behavior is that of the rigid, punitive father, who is in reality acting out the role of Laius, father of Oedipus. Here, more than passive neglect, there is overt rejection and physical or mental cruelty, often rationalized as discipline and training for the child's betterment. Children with that kind of father image have drawn father as an overwhelming figure, often with large hands and long, spiky fingers.

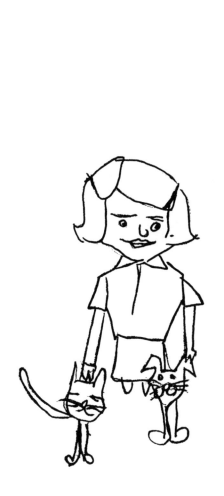

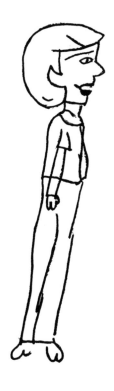

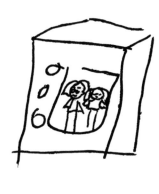

FIGURE 52

Refusal to draw the family

Only among children from broken homes have I met with a flat refusal to draw the family. One embittered boy countered with, "I have no family." But even among these traumatized children, absolute resistance is rare. More commonly, they have drawn a family group in which they have included all their siblings and themselves but omitted their parents (Figure 53).

Where there is reluctance to cooperate, the request to draw a tree may remove the emotional block and pave the way for freer response at another time.

To those who say the drawings are superfluous, that they tell what we already know, I say they tell us more about what we may know.

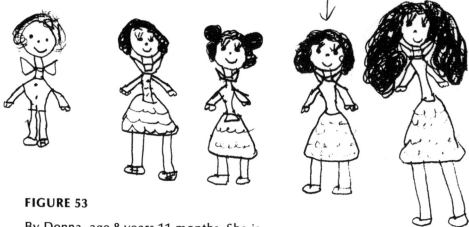

FIGURE 53

By Donna, age 8 years 11 months. She is the fourth from the left. Broken home. All children in temporary shelter. Parents have been omitted from the family drawing.

Geometric figures

Figures 54 is a drawing of human figures by a child of 6 years, currently in foster care because of deteriorating conditions in her own fatherless home.

Her renditions of the human figures are strikingly geometric. The human figure is depersonalized and dehumanized, expressed as an object. This type of drawing expresses an attitude that is cerebrally controlled, rational, unemotional. The viewer's response is accordingly intellectual, not affective.

The child is doing well in first grade. She has formed no close attachments to either the foster family or to her natural mother, who visits sporadically.

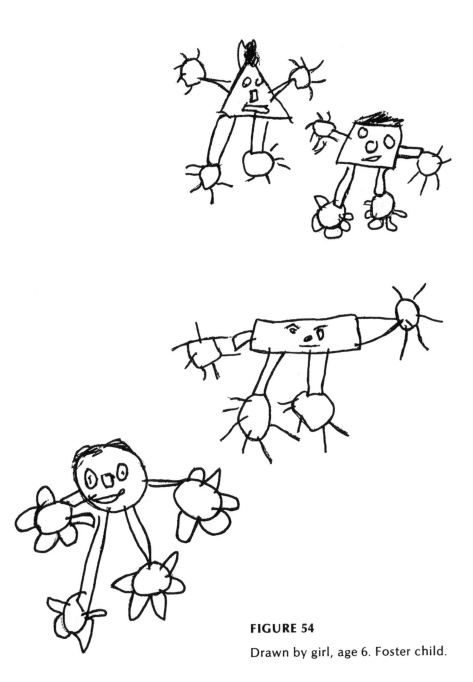

FIGURE 54

Drawn by girl, age 6. Foster child.

Is the drawing a self-image?

Related to this question is the recognition of the reflection in the mirror as a self-image. In an ingenious and fascinating investigation, René Zazzo (1975) sought to determine the sequences that lead to a child's discovery that the mirror is reflecting himself.

At first, the child sees his identical twin through a clear plate glass, which is then replaced by a mirror. Zazzo was able to determine the age at which most children would, on seeing a dark spot on the nose, reach for it on their own rather than on the nose reflected in the mirror. Practically all were successful by age 30 months.

This study led me to reexamine the question of the drawn image: Is it intended or recognized as a self-image?

Reviewing hundreds of drawings made in response to the request "draw a person," a small number spontaneously stated, "That's me"; another small number spontaneously stated that they had drawn a friend; some drew a parent; some, from broken homes, drew a caring grandparent; most drew what appeared to be an adult figure but did not specify either spontaneously or responsively.

In an earlier work (1973), I expressed the belief that the well-adjusted child draws "a concept of humankind rather than just of the Self . . . the Self is included and absorbed." Just as we are unaware of our organ activity until something begins to hurt, "the child who is not tormented by anxiety forgets the Self in a thorough involvement with the fascinating world of persons and things," so that the drawing "is more likely to be a schema that represents a significant adult" or, I might add, a friend. It is a well-known fact that most children will draw their own sex first when asked to draw a person, but that is not the same as drawing themselves.

In my series, the youngest child to spontaneously identify the figure as a self-image was 6 years of age. One boy of 4 years 10 months spontaneously called the figure "mommie"; another boy of 4 years 8 months told me he had drawn his brother. The vast majority were over 8 when they gave the figures a name.

In reviewing a series of drawings of a single human figure by latency children from broken homes, I found no significant difference between boys and girls as regards the choice of subject other than the usual tendency to draw their own sex first, a tendency which, however, diminishes as girls approach puberty and may draw a male figure first. This I have interpreted as an expression of interest rather than identification. Among these children there seems to be an inclination to draw a coeval friend or a caring adult (doctor, nurse, social worker, grandparent) rather than a parent. This fact underscores the importance of close relationships within the peer group and with benevolent caretakers when natural parents are unable or unwilling to assume their expected roles.

In Figures 55 and 56 Joseph has drawn John and John has drawn Joseph.

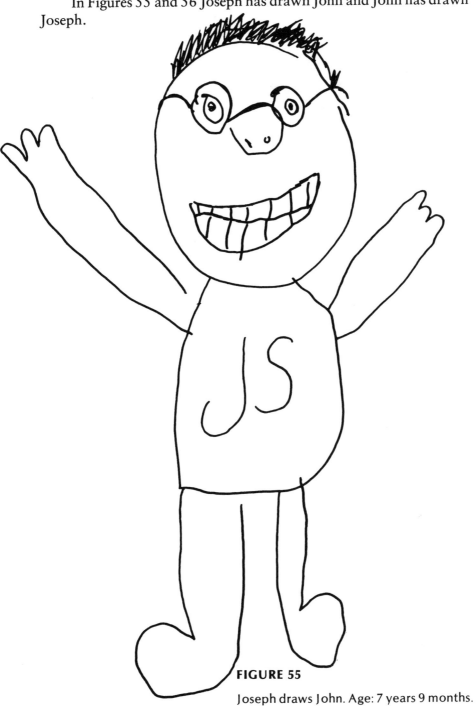

FIGURE 55

Joseph draws John. Age: 7 years 9 months.

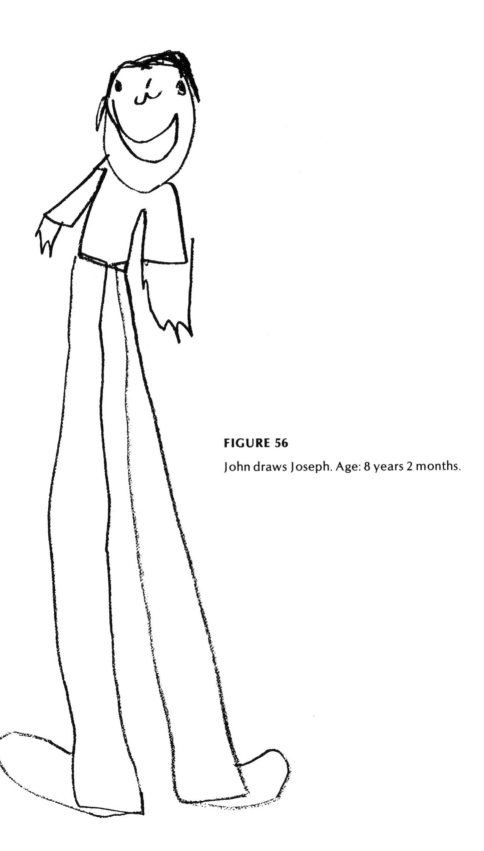

FIGURE 56

John draws Joseph. Age: 8 years 2 months.

8

BODY PARTS

A hierarchy of parts

The term hierarchy is used here to express the order and regularity with which parts of the body appear in drawings by the developing child. It is assumed that in this evolution of the human figure lies the significance with which the child views the body parts.

There is general agreement that the earliest representation is a circle, which three- to four-year-olds will identify spontaneously or responsively as a person or even, more specifically, as a head. Whether this circular pattern comprises the trunk as well (Arnheim, 1964; Britsch, 1926), the fact remains that it is into this primordial circle that the child will add eyes, mouth, and nose. Later, a smaller circle beneath the original one will clearly indicate the trunk. For reasons expounded at some length in an earlier publication (Di Leo, 1970), I believe that the young child, intuitively and validly, is most strikingly impressed by that part of the human anatomy that actually, as well as symbolically, is by far the most representative part of a person.

In the ensuing discussion, I have selected the head, eyes, and upper and lower extremities for special attention because of their predominant role in bringing the child into relationship with the outer world of persons and things.

The head

> "Before constructing the vital
> organs, Nature forms the part
> that is the seat of intellect."
> Leonardo da Vinci

Sir Julian Huxley (1961) refers to the head as the "dominant guiding region of the body," the receptor of information as well as the central coordinating organ.

Edmund S. Crelin (1973), anatomist, states that the head accounts for one-half of the total length in a two-month fetus, and one-quarter of the crown-to-heel length in a newborn; that it outstrips all other body parts in rapidity of growth and attainment of full development, reaching 90 percent of its adult size by the fifth year of age.

With uncanny intuition, the child has selected for prime attention the part of us that from embryonic life assumed, and usually continues to retain, a primacy over the rest of the organism.

Apart from its preeminent role in mental and emotional life, the head is invested with symbolic attributes that find expression in graphic representation. Typically, in drawings by preschool children, the head is disproportionately large as it dominates the figure (Figure 57). But as the child matures and drawings become more realistic—usually by age seven or eight—the human figure and its parts assume more objective proportions and the head size is about one-eighth of the crown-to-heel length in the standing adult figure. How is one to interpret striking variations in head size?

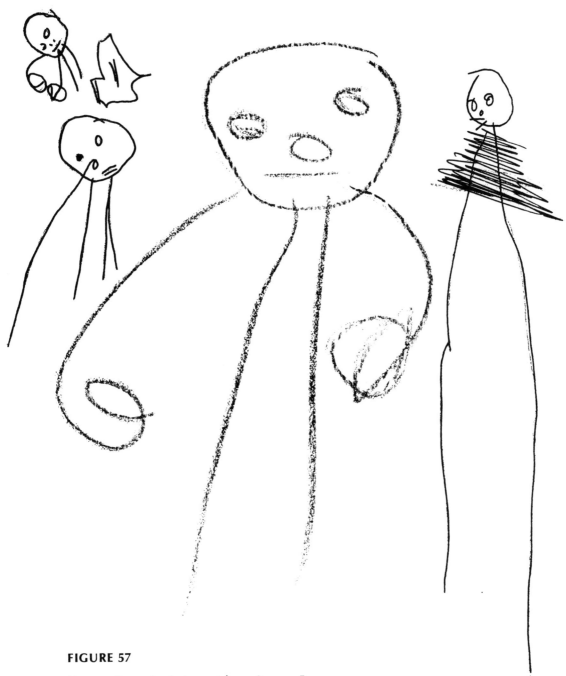

FIGURE 57

Human figure by J. A., a girl age 3 years 5
months, of superior intelligence.

Huge head

This striking variation may be seen in drawings by the mentally retarded as they continue to think and act at developmentally lower levels than chronological age (Figure 58).

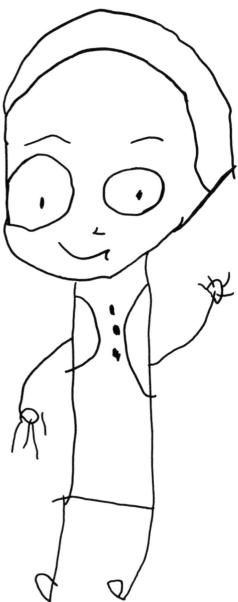

FIGURE 58

By a boy, age 12 years 3 months. Mentally retarded. Undergoing treatment for phenylketonuria. The huge head is typically seen in drawings by much younger children of average intelligence.

The head is often seen, especially in Renaissance art, as representative of the whole person. Only rarely is any other part of the body so used, whereas countless seraphs and cherubs are depicted as simply head and wings. Young children will often draw the head alone, with eyes, nose, and mouth, to effectively represent the person, as in Figure 59 by a boy of 8, who was requested to draw his family.

In the child of average or superior intelligence, an excessively large head may express focus on what is regarded as the seat of a physical or psychological dysfunction.

Large heads are drawn by school-age children with dyslexia in attributing the learning difficulty to some malfunction located in the head.

One might be tempted to view the large head frequently seen in drawings by schizophrenic persons as just another manifestation of regression in service of the ego. But that is an oversimplification that does not take into account the qualitative and substantial difference between the disordered thought processes of the patient and those of the normal child, though both draw humans with huge heads.

The cephalopod drawn typically by 5- and 6-year-olds expresses the primacy of the head as intuitively perceived by the young child. Fascination with the head and its features begins early in human life. Nothing attracts the month-old baby more than the human face. Beyond babyhood, the child views the part of the body that sees, talks, hears, eats, laughs and grimaces as a worthy representative of what really counts above the rest. Awareness of the essential functions within the trunk is an intellectual concept that will come later when the child adds a smaller circle beneath the dominating head.

The huge head drawn by the mental patient has a far more complex meaning. I believe it to be well expressed by Halbreich (1979), who interprets the cephalopod as a depersonalized mask. Head and body are fused in an attempt to gain control over the terrifying feelings that emanate from a symbolic decapitation in which mind and body go their separate ways. The patient identifies with the cephalopodic, depersonalized mask; it is unchanging, ritualistic, and archetypal. But the process is a retreat into a symbol-fantasy world.

In the young child, the cephalopod is a developmental phase; in the patient, it is an attempt to arrest change. In the first, the process is dynamic; in the other, static.

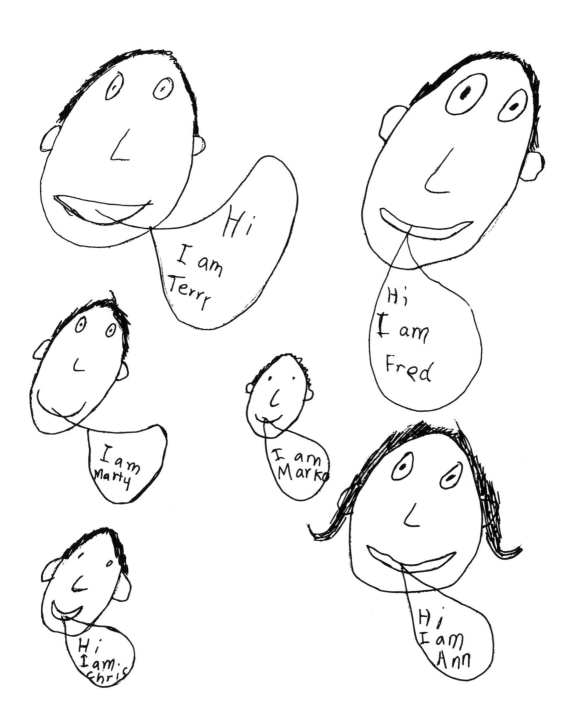

FIGURE 59

Drawn by boy, age 8. His family.

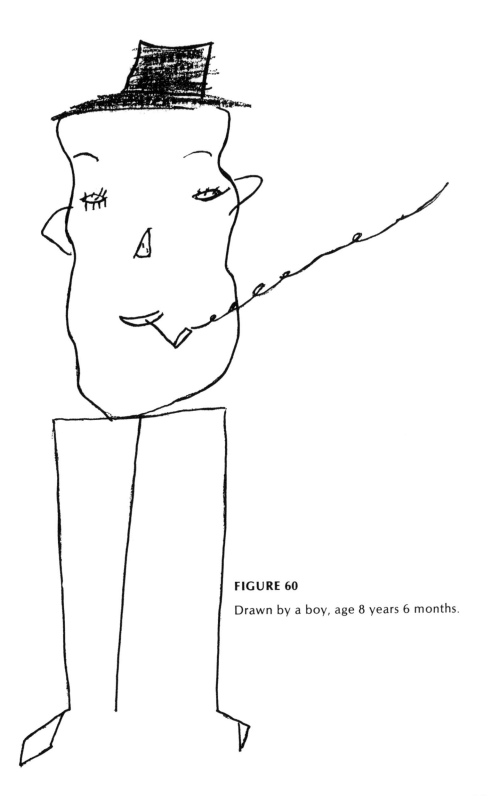

FIGURE 60

Drawn by a boy, age 8 years 6 months.

FIGURE 61

By a boy age 8. Stanford-Binet: mental age and Goodenough correspond. I.Q. 89.

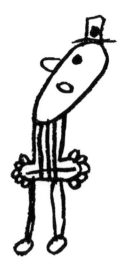

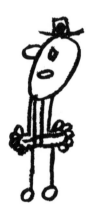

The eye

Veneration of the sun as the supreme power, source of light, giver and sustainer of life was the central religious practice of many ancient cultures. Rich in symbols, Egyptian mythology chose the eye to represent Horus, the great sun deity. The eye figures prominently in the art of ancient Egypt. In paintings and reliefs, the face is characteristically in profile, but the eye always faces front, looking directly at the viewer and emphatically outlined in black in both paintings and statuary.

It is through the eye that light and image enter the body. And it is the eye that is destined to displace its mother, touch, as the prime medium for our contact with the world outside. Its function, though primarily receptive, is far from passive, for it is able to select what it will transmit to cerebral awareness.

Belief in emanations from the eye is still current, especially among those who hang amulets round their children's necks for protection against the evil eye. But it was not superstition that led Leonardo da Vinci to recognize the beguiling power of a maiden's eye. References to emanations from the eye abound in the works of great writers as well as poets, as when Petrarca recalls "si dolce lume uscia dagli occhi suoi" (so sweet was the light that shone from her eyes).

Expression derives largely from action of the muscles that surround the eye. Its intrinsic fascinating effect lies in its sparkling reflection of light, in the beauty of its colors, and in children, in the innocent look of its large, wide-open pupil. But there is more to the eye than its physical attributes.

It is no wonder, then, that the eye receives so much attention in art, psychology, and in human affairs.

"Even in earliest infancy, nothing will engage the baby's attention like the human face; but within the face it is the eyes that spellbind, and activity subsides." This observation by Di Leo (1970) and other clinicians, based upon long experience in studying the behavioral development of young infants, has been confirmed by Haith, Moore, and Bergman (1977). By an ingenious use of TV cameras, videotape, and sophisticated statistical analysis, these authors studied the scanning patterns of 24 infants in response to mothers' and strangers' faces. The infants were divided into three age groups—3 to 5, 7, and 9 to 11 weeks. Eye contact and fixation were compared with fixation on nose, mouth, and contours (hairline, cheeks, chin, ears). The adult faces were still, moving, and then talking.

The results are most interesting, though they but confirm what has been known clinically. There was no significant difference between the responses to mother and to stranger. It is, in fact, known that infants do not recognize mother's face before they are closer to four months of age. Most of the infants in the first age group (57.4 percent) were attracted by the contours. But by age 7 weeks, the eyes became the predominantly attractive facial components to 54.8 percent, and to 48.9 percent at 9 to 11 weeks of age. The preference for eyes has been attributed to their movement, color, and lustre. But then how does one explain the fact that mouth, teeth, and lips failed to compete successfully for the infant's attention when the adult presented a talking face. In fact, the infant's attention to eyes was enhanced when the adult began to talk.

The authors of this study relate their findings to perceptual and social development, postulating that by 7 weeks "the face has changed its status from a mere collection of elements to a meaningful entity or perceptual configuration and that from that time on, the eyes have "acquired signal value in social interaction."

The importance of eye contact in the establishment of social rapport between infant and caretaker is well known, as is the distressing prognostic import of persistent failure to establish or sustain eye contact. It is indeed gratifying to learn that another clinical finding has received scientific confirmation.

Even before he is 2 months old, the infant will stare at the caretaker's eyes, seemingly transfixed, as movement of arms and legs comes to a halt. Persistent failure to establish and sustain eye contact is one of the earliest signs of a disordered psyche.

In the child's initial recognizable attempts to portray the human figure, eyes are the first and most prominent features to be added to the primordial circle of the head. Emphasis by making the eyes excessively large has been observed in drawings by suspicious and paranoid persons, but in the young child, large eyes are simply an expression of the importance that is understandably attached to this most wonderful part of our person (Figure 62).

The association of eyes with sexual arousal, voyeurism, guilt, and shame may be reflected in unusual treatment of the eyes in drawings by adolescents who may draw eyes without pupils (blind eyes), abnormally tiny, hidden by dark glasses, or may even omit them altogether. Guilt over incest leads Oedipus to gouge out his eyes that they "might never look again on what they had no right to see. . . . "

Cosmetic embellishment of the eyes is often seen in female figures drawn by adolescent girls. Eyes drawn by boys are simpler—just plain and functional. One is reminded of the adage, "L'uomo ha due occhi per vedere, la donna due occhi per essere vista" (A man's eyes are for looking; a woman's for being looked at). Figure 63 is drawn by a male, Figure 64 by a female.

Many of us feel with Marcel Proust that what shines in those reflecting discs is not just due to their material composition. Poets tell how love enters through the eyes. The visual interplay between persons is not just a matter of optics.

FIGURE 62

Huge eyes are commonly seen in drawings by young children, as in this figure by a bright, secure girl of 4 years 7 months living in her own home in an intact family.

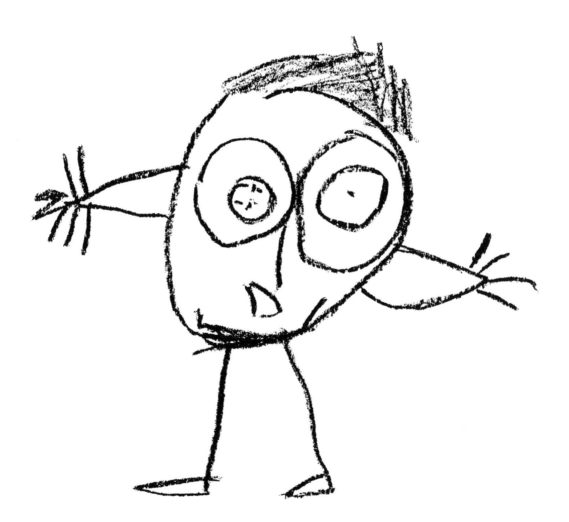

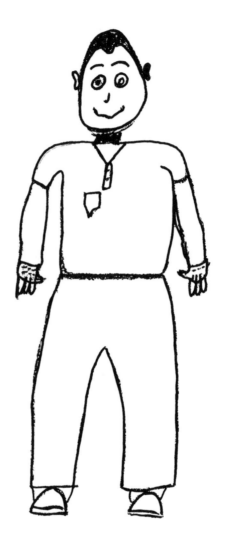

FIGURE 63

Drawn by boy, age 12.

FIGURE 64

Drawn by girl, age 11.

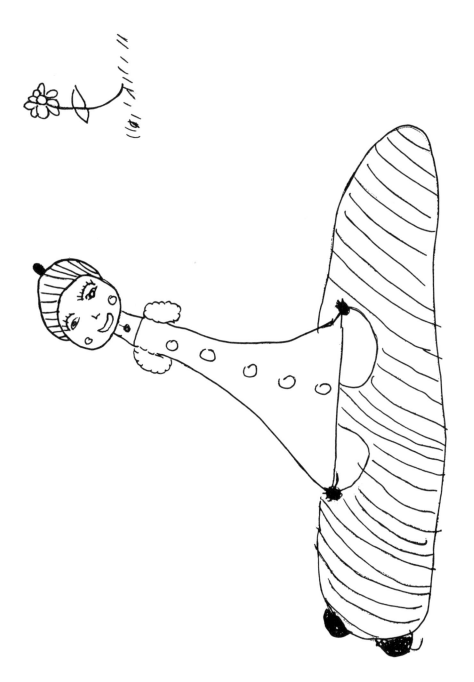

Arms and hands

Touch is the mother of the senses. It was through the tactile stimulus to our lips that we first made contact and began to relate to the world beyond the womb. Eventually, hands and fingers will become the chief agents for making direct contact and even for communicating by gesture and sign.

It is through touch that we may receive or bestow affection or punishment. Arms and hands bless or condemn, give or take away. Symbolism of the upper extremities is often manifest in the form, dimensions, or absence of these parts so active in the life of relationships. Accordingly, attention to how arms, hands, and fingers are portrayed may help understand behavior that often overlies fear, timidity, or hostility and aggression.

But before attempting an interpretation, it is essential to refer to the developmental sequences that typify evolution of the human figure in the vast majority of children. One does not expect to see arms at age 4. Their absence becomes increasingly significant beyond age 6, and surely so at age 10. The same applies to their dimensions and to their point of attachment. We do not expect school-age children to continue drawing arms that come out of heads or out of legs (unless they are pulling our leg).

Figure 65 is by a boy of 6 years 8 months. He is from a broken home. He is described as withdrawn and suspicious, traits that are expressed by the absence of hands and arms and by large eyes directed sideways.

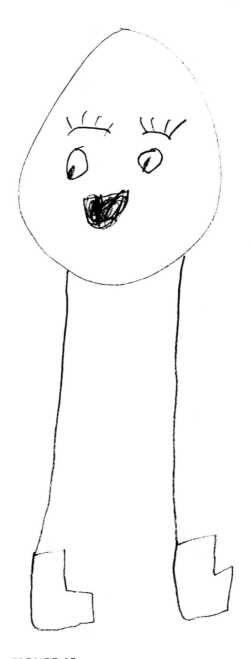

FIGURE 65

By boy, age 6 years 8 months. Suspicion and inaction.

In Figure 66 by Brenda, age 10 years 7 months, there is a clear relationship between Brenda's personality and her art. She is an intelligent but unmotivated child; cooperative, but with a tendency to passivity, preferring solitude. The figures have no arms or hands; they can do nothing. The only resistance encountered occurred when she was asked to draw the members of her family doing something. She invoked inability to portray action.

The drawing, made in a practically continuous line, displays artistic ability and aesthetic sense. The careful manner and accurate meeting of lines manifest the control that is an outstanding trait of her personality. The rigid stance of her figures, despite their smiles, may be interpreted as defense.

The origin of her lack of motivation is traceable to disruptive forces in the home.

FIGURE 66

By Brenda, age 10 years 7 months. Static, passive, stereotyped figures. No arms. Unstable feet.

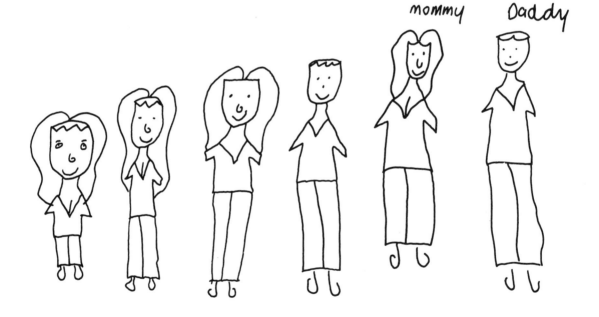

The ear

In drawings, ears may be omitted or made huge or emphasized by heavy pressure of the writing instrument. What significance may be attributed to such variations? As the organ of hearing, one would expect to see unusual attention to its portrayal by persons who are hard of hearing and by those who experience auditory hallucinations or ideas of reference.

In my long years as a consultant at a school for the deaf, I have not found consistent emphasis on ears in drawings by the hearing-impaired. A few drew themselves with a hearing aid. As regards treatment of ears, most could not be distinguished on that basis from normal controls.

The interpretation of conspicuous ears as an expression of paranoid, suspicious attitudes or hallucinatory disturbances has been noted by various investigators, notably Machover, Hammer, and Griffith and Peyman. These latter investigators, however, found a positive correlation between ear emphasis and ideas of reference only when they relied on behavioral criteria and not on psychiatric labels. (Ear emphasis as one of the distinguishing symbols [lakṣanā] of Buddha is mentioned in Chapter 1).

Absence of ears is typical of human figures drawn by preschool children and is simply due to immaturity in the developing concept of the image. Ears are often but not consistently absent from drawings by deaf or hearing-impaired school-age children. Drawing one's own defect into a human figure does occur at times; but more often the child tends to draw a desired or idealized image, just as obese persons tend to draw a slender silhouette.

Anatomical concepts

The Inside-of-the-Body test offers an opportunity to assess the subject's perception of organ systems in health and disease (Brumback, 1977).

The heart and brain are emphasized in most drawings by school-age children. Other organ systems appear in time. Boys are more likely to stress bone and muscular structures to a greater degree in drawings than girls. Boys are also more prone to draw the genito-urinary system. Neuromuscular or cardiac disorder may be represented overtly or symbolically in drawings by some patients.

In general, the child's concept of the internal structure of the body is greatly influenced by what is taught at school, thereby placing limitations on the value of this test.

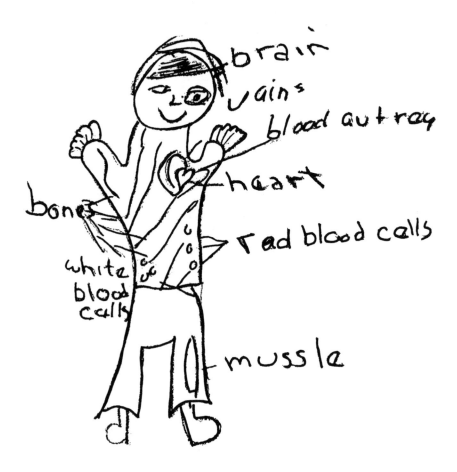

FIGURE 67

Human anatomy according to Linda, age
15, having just been promoted to tenth
grade.

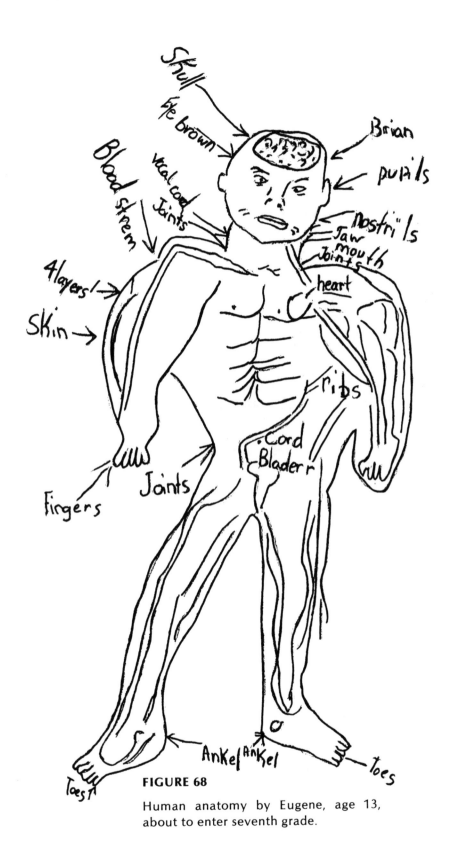

FIGURE 68

Human anatomy by Eugene, age 13, about to enter seventh grade.

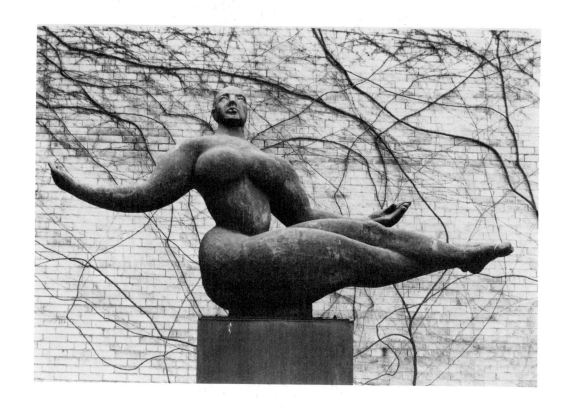

PLATE I

Gaston Lachaise. *Floating Figure* (1927). Bronze (cast 1935). 51 ¾ ″ × 8′. Collection, The Museum of Modern Art, New York. Given anonymously in memory of the artist.

9

SEX DIFFERENCES AND SEX ROLES IN WESTERN SOCIETY AS PERCEIVED BY CHILDREN

Early depiction of sex differences

It is well known that the first attempts that preschool children make to depict the difference between male and female are the endowment of the female figure with longer hair. This fact is evident today as in the past despite the visual spectacle of interchangeable hair styles.

In the garden of the Museum of Modern Art, I was one day admiring the statues, when my attention was drawn to a child of four displaying admirable interest in modern art and particularly in a work by Gaston Lachaise. Turning to his mother and pointing to the figure, he remarked, "Mommy, look at that man" (Plate I). The figure, abundantly endowed with secondary female characteristics, has closely cropped hair on her head. I do not know the child's I.Q., but he was quite alert and articulate. My informal evaluation was that he was not retarded.

We see the attribution of more hair to the female figure well beyond the preschool years, quite apart from the erotic symbolism that is expressed by hair in drawings by adolescents and adults.

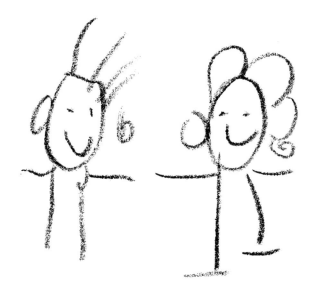

FIGURE 69

"My father and my mother" by a boy of 6
years 4 months.

FIGURE 70

Drawing of family by a dyslexic boy of 7 years 10 months. The figure without arms is his permissive father. Male and female are distinguished by their hair.

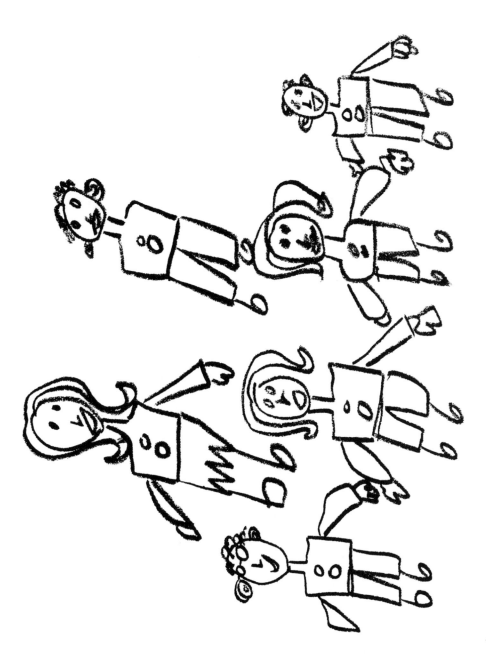

Sex differences as perceived by school-age children

In Figure 71 a girl of 10 has portrayed her own sex in response to "draw a person." Hair, eye detail, mouth treatment, breasts, and clothing typically proclaim her awareness of sex and role.

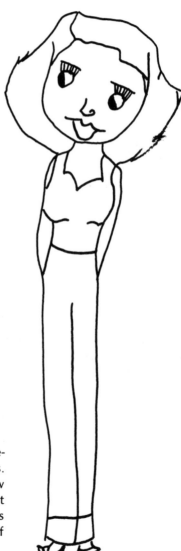

FIGURE 71

Drawn by a girl of 10. Hispanic. The female figure is wearing pants, high heels. Abundant hair, eye lashes, cupid's bow lips, and well-rounded breasts suggest strong identification with mother. Hands behind the back suggest youthful lack of confidence in dealing with people.

By contrast, Figure 72, drawn by a boy of 10, clearly portrays interests and aspirations of boys who assume their traditional role. (This boy is left-handed. He has crossed over, showing the left as the pitching arm. The arms and hands are prominent, hair is short, with no embellishment of eyes and mouth. Motion has been imparted to the ball).

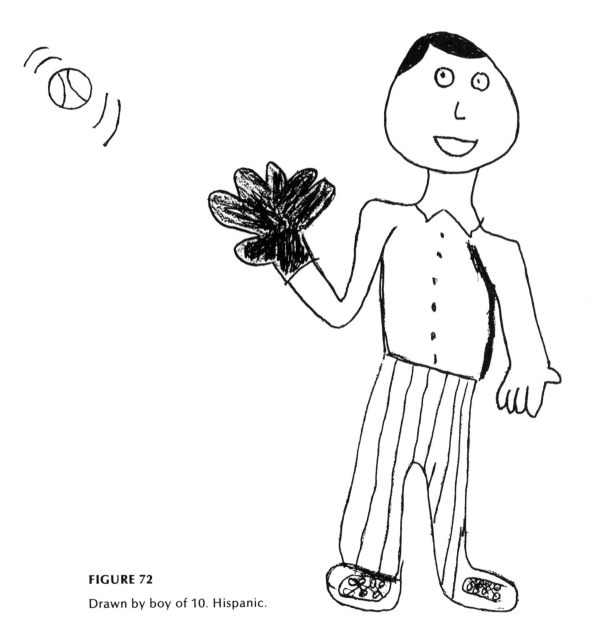

FIGURE 72

Drawn by boy of 10. Hispanic.

The latency child is growing

"Tears had not yet touched my breast,
nor broken my sleep, and what was not
in me seemed as a miracle in others . . .
but then I grew, I knew."
Francesco Petrarca

In Figure 73, by a boy of 10, there are children: one with a bicycle, another watching CBS news. There are also pictures of children: two arguing in a badly hung picture, and in the "love room" one depicting the artist embracing his favorite sisters. Also in this room is a light bulb (symbol of warmth) and on a love seat, with a heart over each, are two adults kissing.

FIGURE 73

By a boy, age 10.

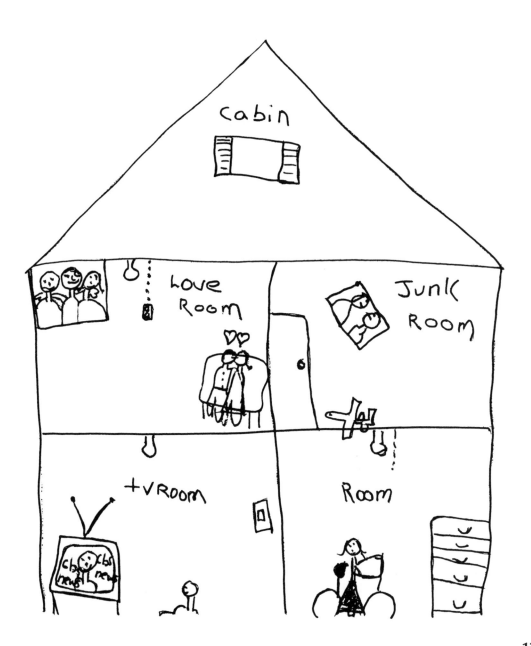

Sex roles in western society

To this day, despite valiant efforts to achieve social justice, traditional distinction of sex roles persists at least as an undercurrent in human affairs. Separation of sex roles is evident in the drawings of children. Too young and candid to disguise their attitudes and feelings, they openly reveal how they have been influenced to accept what is considered proper to each sex.

A look at the past, with the hope of not repeating its blunders, will clearly reveal the deeply entrenched conviction that the difference in sex is almost a difference in species. The separation that marked life in the ancient world is too well known to require repetition. More appropriate to our time is the persistence of attitudes expressed during the Renaissance. Leon Battista Alberti's *I Libri della Famiglia* is the richest source of information in this regard.

He tells how a wise father would not concern himself with things that are woman's domain; that children (he always speaks of boys) should be segregated from all feminine activities; how the role of the wife is to preserve what the husband brings home. With regard to choice of a wife, the young men are advised to marry well after 25 and to choose a young girl so that she will more easily learn to accept the husband's habits. Preferably, she should have a great number of brothers as she may then be like her mother and produce many sons, the purpose of marriage being primarily to perpetuate the father in his sons, and then to have a steady, faithful, obedient companion. The wife shall have domain over the household but she may not see family records and books. Being very modest, she will not care to know more than is her business.

When the child draws the family in action (K-F-D)—each member doing something—mother and daughter are often pictured at household chores (cooking, cleaning, serving at table), while father is involved in more "dignified" activities, such as reading the newspaper, watching TV, drinking, smoking. Only occasionally will he be doing something useful, such as hammering a nail or tinkering with the car. Brother is usually playing ball or doing homework. These stereotypes are seen in drawings by girls as well as boys.

The roles assigned to male and female members persist in the minds of children despite the fact that mother may be engaged in work outside the home, while today's father may be participating actively in the preparation of meals and in the maintenance of a clean home.

Boys in particular will draw their sisters but not themselves doing household work, possibly from fear of ridicule, or probably to show that ordinary household activities are for females, while sports and intellectual activities are more properly for males.

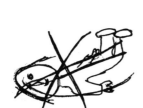

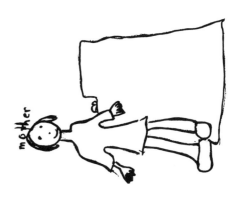

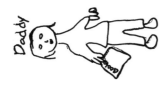

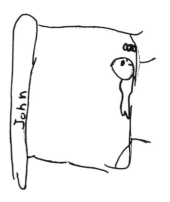

FIGURE 74

Drawn by a girl, age 11 years. "Daddy is reading a book. Mother is in the kitchen."

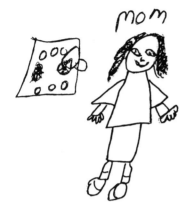

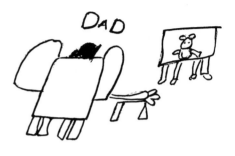

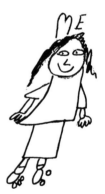

Carmen

FIGURE 75

Family drawn by girl, age 10 years 2
months (K-F-D).
"Mother is cooking rice"
"Dad is watching TV, resting his foot"
"That's me, outside, skating"

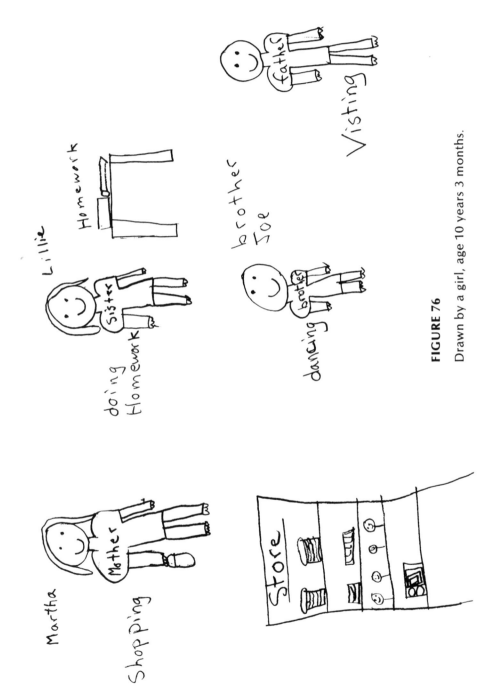

FIGURE 76

Drawn by a girl, age 10 years 3 months.

137

FIGURE 77

Drawn by a boy of 8. He is playing with a yo-yo. Father walks the dog. Mother with her shopping cart provides food (love).

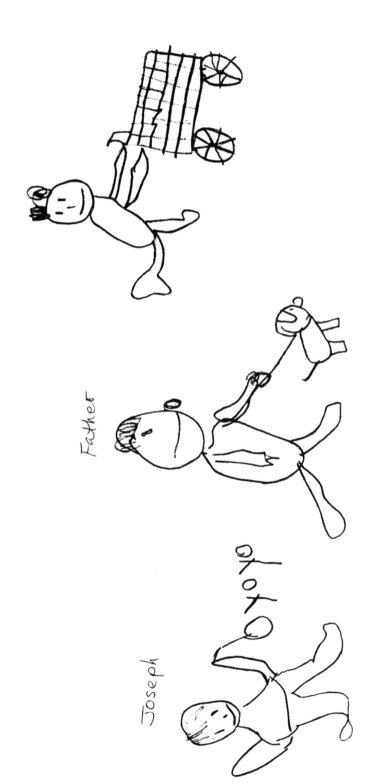

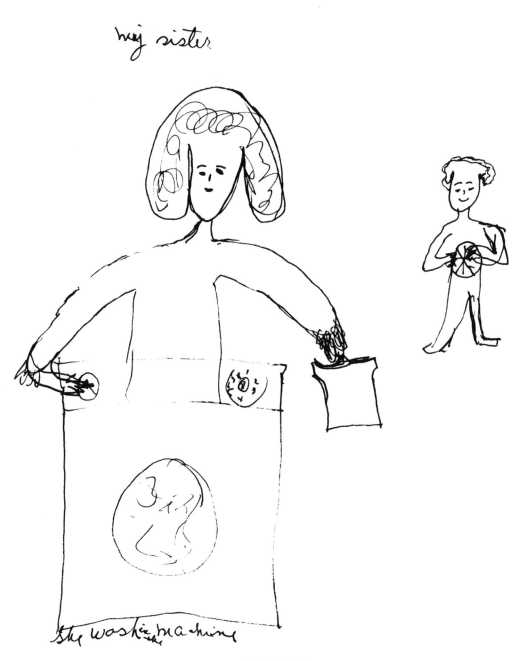

my sister

the washing machine

FIGURE 78

Drawn by a 23-year-old retarded female.
While the female is washing, the male
plays with his ball.

FIGURE 79

Drawn by a girl, age 11 years. Father is sleeping. The children are reading. Mother is the only one working.

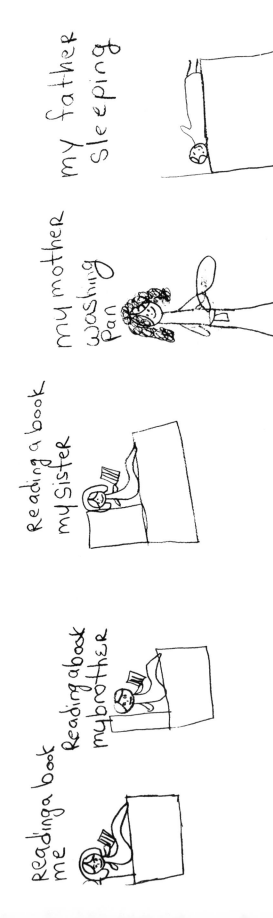

It should be remembered, however, that symbolism may predominate in the drawings of latency children and that the mother preparing and serving food is likely to symbolize her as dispensing affection.

Furthermore, it is worthy of note that drawings made by American children during the 1980s reveal an increasing tendency to blur the distinctions that separate female from male. The sexes as represented are generally indistinguishable by their clothing, and women are depicted engaged in sports and leisure activities. Hair remains as a persistent differentiating item despite the prevalence of unisex tonsorial art.

Emancipation

Children's drawings are beginning to show changes in the perception of sex roles. Females are portrayed taking over activities traditionally reserved for males. In Figure 80 mother is piloting a plane. In Figure 81 mother is relaxing.

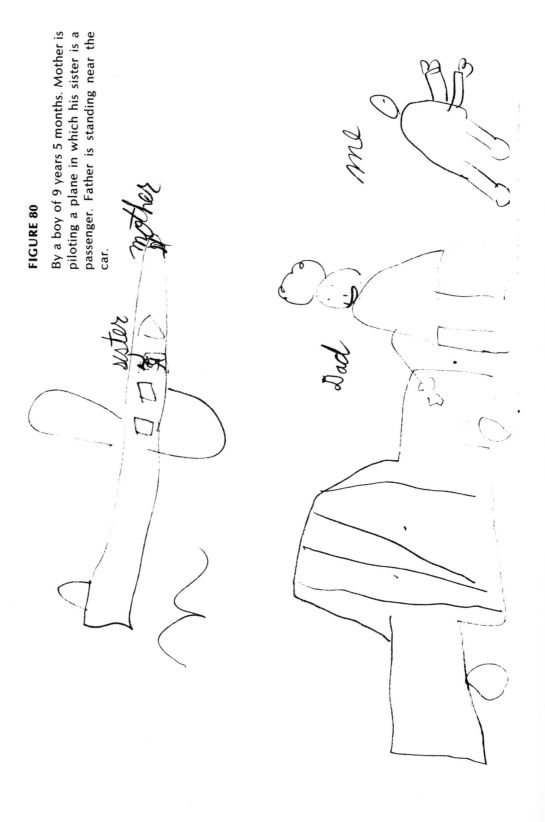

FIGURE 80

By a boy of 9 years 5 months. Mother is piloting a plane in which his sister is a passenger. Father is standing near the car.

FIGURE 81

Drawn by a girl, age 9 years 10 months.

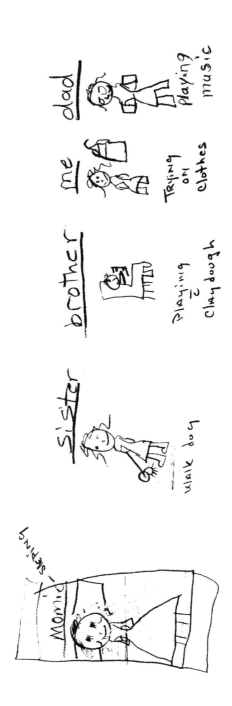

144

FIGURE 82

Rebellion against the stereotyped sex role is evident in this drawing by Sandra, age 14. Though drawing her mother cooking and her father reading, she has pictured herself wearing a karate belt and "flipping" someone. She shares her brothers' enthusiasm for sports and has added a baseball game to her picture. The parents are given their traditional roles, but she has other inclinations. Mara is playing with a doll, but she is only 3.

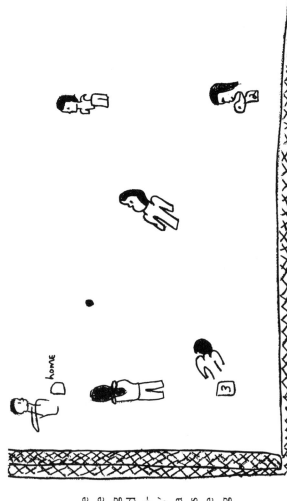
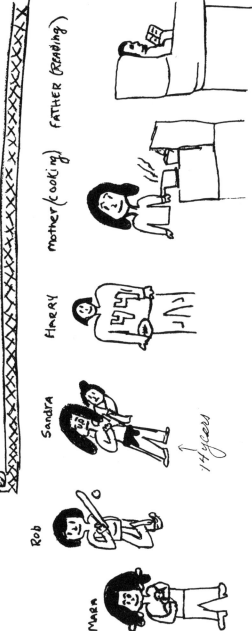

Most females are shown wearing pants.

I have no drawings in which men are wearing dresses.

I was about to say that I had never seen a male serving food, washing dishes, or cleaning the rooms. Only once had I seen father doing what might be credited as a household task: he was hammering a nail into the wall. But then, the unexpected occurred. Albert, age 11 years 9 months, made a K-F-D in which Mom is resting while Dad is cooking. He is the only one working. Sister and her friend are watching TV by remote control (Figure 83). Albert commented, "Father is cooking a piece of chicken. He has a machete to show he killed it."

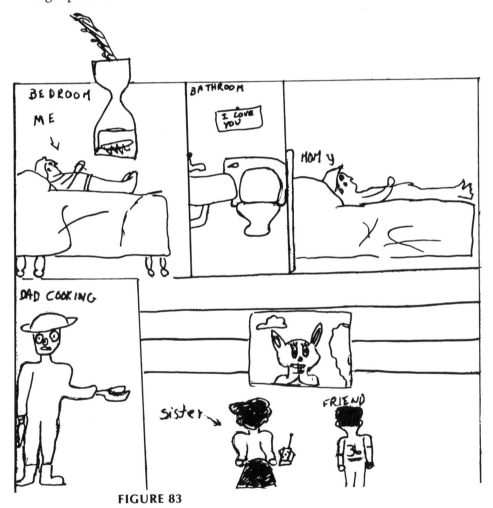

FIGURE 83

By Albert, age 11 years 9 months. Sister and friend watching TV. This is the only drawing I have in which the father is cooking.

10

LATERALITY AND ITS EFFECTS ON DRAWING

Early evidences of handedness

During the first three months after birth, infants lying on their backs will assume an asymmetrical posture known as the tonic neck reflex. The head is turned to one side, the arm on that side is extended while the other arm is flexed close to the shoulder so that the posture resembles a fencing stance. This tends to channelize vision towards the outstretched hand, thereby paving the way for eye-hand coordination (Gesell and Amatruda, 1941).

Many infants display a consistent "preference" for either the right or left orientation of this early, conspicuous postural reflex, as in this normal 12-week infant (Figure 84).

Eye and hand

Associated with handedness is a homolateral eyedness so that hand and eye function in unison on the same side for greater efficiency in most persons. Underlying the homolaterality of hand and eye (some

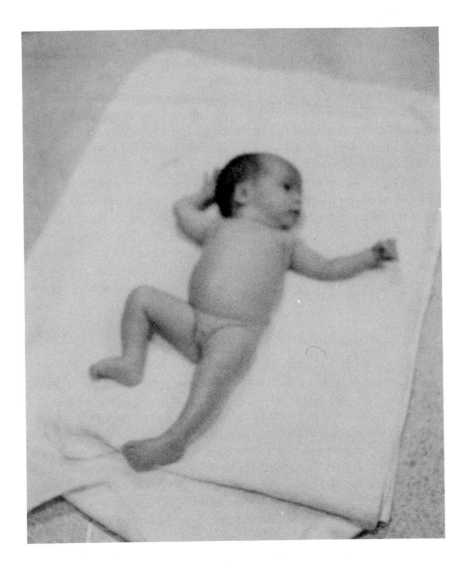

FIGURE 84

would have the eye guiding the hand) is the dominance of one or the other contralateral motor area in the brain. This contralateral control of movement is the result of a crossing of the motor pathways at the base of the brain, so that the left motor area controls the movements of the right side of the body and vice-versa. There is, however, an incomplete separation of the two sides of the brain. Otherwise, we would be functioning as two separate action systems.

The dependence of right- or left-handedness upon corresponding leads from the left or right cerebrum indicates the folly of trying to transform sinistrality into the more usual right-handedness. As with other structural and physiological characteristics of the body, cerebral dominance is genetically induced.

Incidentally, mention may be made of what Trevor-Roper calls a "full-blooded psychoanalytic approach" that would interpret a convergent squint as related to the baby's need to focus on mother's breast. Transient squint is common in infants during the first three months and is observed as well in those who have never been near a woman's breast. I have seen myriads of mother-deprived infants during my 35 years at the New York Foundling Hospital; they, too, showed transient squint.

Directionality and profile orientation

The overwhelming majority of people are right-handed. In some left-handed individuals familial sinistrality is demonstrable; in others it is not.

In the past, environmental pressures forced the conversion from sinistrality. One factor in this country was the imposition of the Palmer Method of calligraphy with its insistence on clockwise circles, entailing an unnatural movement for those who were left-handed—hence the need to shift to the right. (If a child is asked to make simultaneous rotating movements of the two hands, it will become readily apparent that the right hand will move clockwise, while the left will rotate counterclockwise.)

The present generation of young persons, having been spared ill-considered interference with their genetically-induced natural bent, have retained their natural left-handed preference. Even so, the incidence of sinistrality is strikingly low, probably about 10 percent.

How does this affect drawing? Let us first consider directionality. It is essential to distinguish between kinesthetic drawing (scribbling), which characterizes the earlier period during which the child of two or three makes circles and skeins as the eye delights in seeing what the hand is making, and the later period of representational drawing in which the hand obeys the eye.

In kinesthetic drawing, direction of the circles will depend upon the hand used. The right hand following its natural bent will rotate clockwise, the left counterclockwise. The observer can detect it by watching the movement, as well as by examining its record on paper: pressure on the crayon will tend to taper off as circles are completed. The eye follows the hand.

As the child matures, drawing becomes increasingly representational; now it is the eye that guides the hand. This shift is most evident when children draw profiles. In drawing a profile, the right hand moves from the top down in a counterclockwise direction allowing clear vision of what is being drawn, as well as what has been drawn. The left hand will draw the profile also from the top down but in a clockwise direction permitting unobstructed view of what has been and is being drawn.

In both, the natural directionality that prevailed during the kinesthetic period when the hand was followed by the eye is now reversed, as it is the eye that guides the hand in representational drawing. As a result, profiles drawn by the right hand face left; those drawn by the left hand face right. Therein lies an explanation for the striking fact that 80 to 90 percent of profiles are drawn facing left.

In my opinion, handedness is the prime determinant of profile orientation.

Handedness as detected from drawings

In some infants, first evidence of laterality appears as early as six months, when they begin to reach out regularly with one or the other hand, a tendency that presages the eventual emergence of left- or right-handedness. This writer has observed the consistent sequence of left tonic neck reflex, left-hand preference at six months, left-hand scribbling at 15 months, and definite predominance of left hand in all fine motor activity through childhood, youth, and adulthood. This was seen in but a small number of thousands of children who were followed, but when it occurs, it is quite striking. Most children do not show that degree of consistency until they are five.

When children begin to scribble, usually at about 15 months, one can tell from viewing the scribble whether it was made by the right or left hand (Figure 85 and 86). The slant tells the hand used.

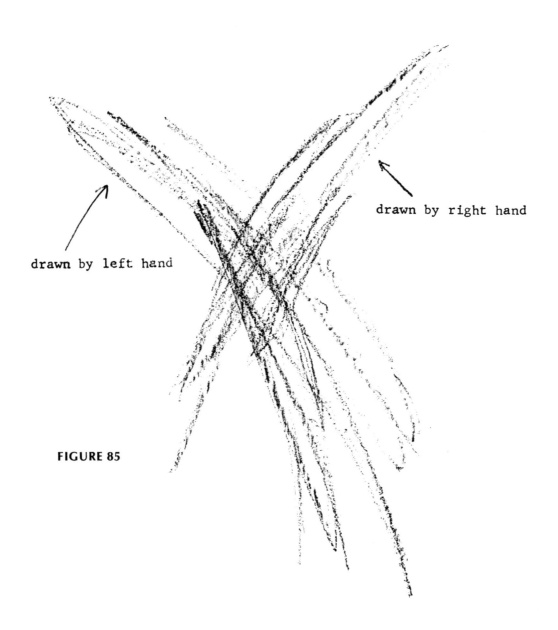

drawn by right hand

drawn by left hand

FIGURE 85

FIGURE 86

Kinesthetic drawing by a girl of 23 months. She first scribbled with her right hand and then switched to her left. The slant indicates the hand used.

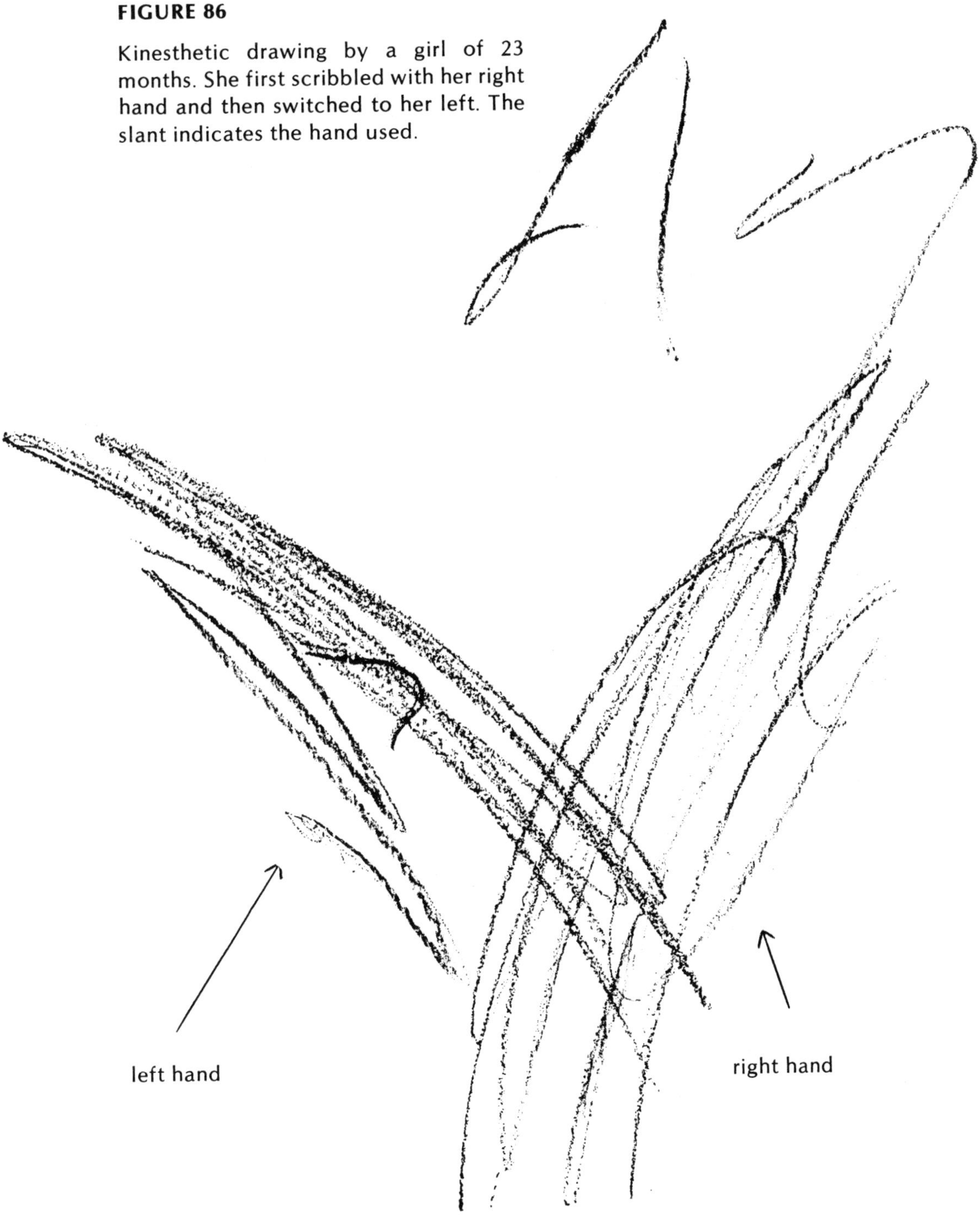

left hand

right hand

Persistence of manual laterality

Figures 87 through Figure 91 comprise a series of drawings by a girl of superior intelligence. Handedness was apparent during early infancy and has persisted unwaveringly into adulthood. Specimens are presented from an early spontaneous scribble at 19 months through nursery and early grades, marked by intense graphic activity.

Shown are:

at 19 months—left-handed scribble
at 3 years 5 months—human figure
at 4 years 3 months—reversal of letters
at 4 years 10 months—reversal of some numbers
at 7 years—drawing of father. Profile facing right is typical orientation by sinistrals.

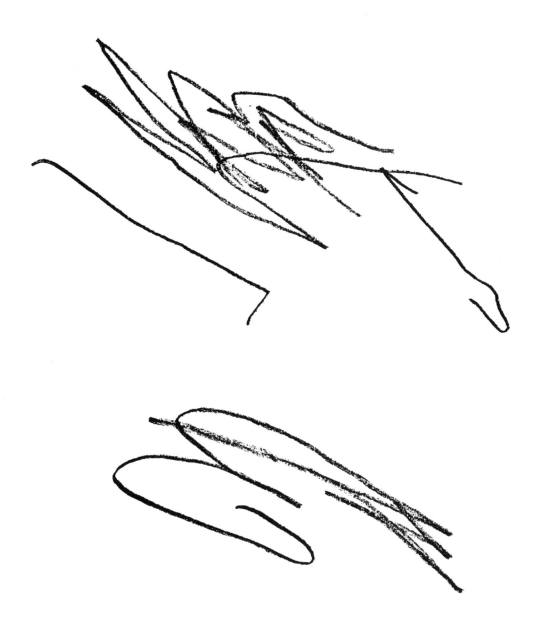

FIGURE 87

Drawn by J. A. at age 19 months. The direction of the spontaneous scribbles indicates that they were made with the left hand.

FIGURE 88

Human figure as drawn by J. A., a bright girl of 3 years 5 months. The drawing was made with her left hand. The circle representing the head was drawn counterclockwise; pressure on the crayon was more intense at the start and slackened as the circle was completed.

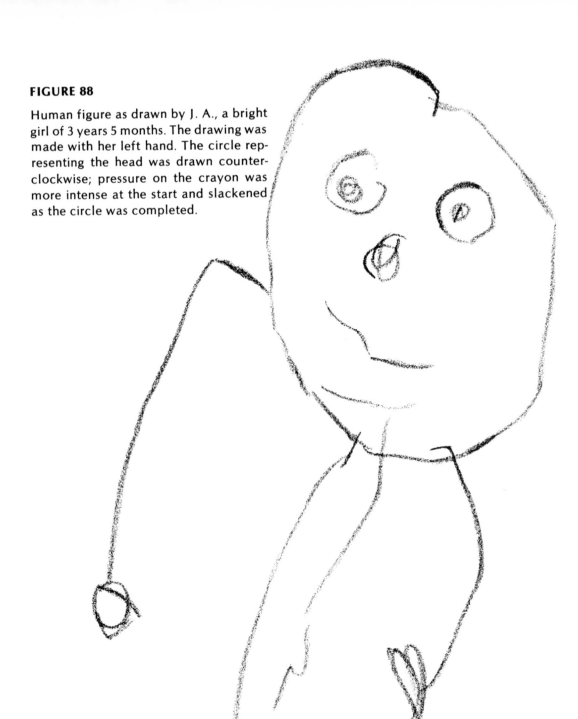

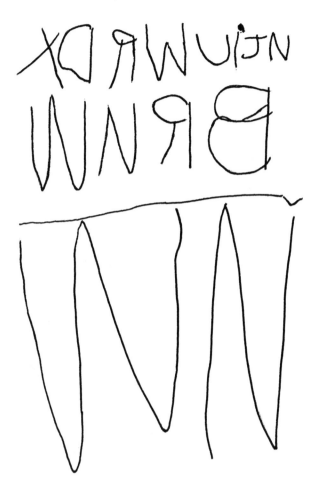

FIGURE 89

Drawn by J. A., who is now 4 years 3 months of age. She is beginning to write. The direction is from right to left. B, R, D, and J are reversed. Numbers and letters with a circular component are those more likely to be reversed: 2, 3, 6, 9, B, D, R, J, P.

FIGURE 90

Drawn by J. A. at 4 years 10 months. Decidedly left-handed child. Superior intelligence.

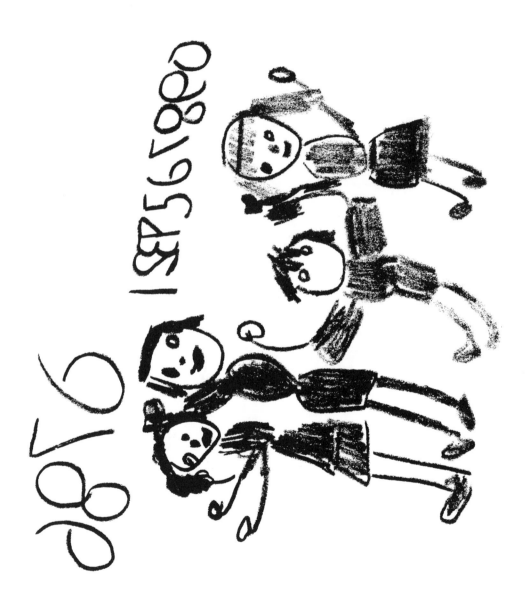

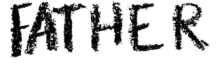

FIGURE 91

Drawn by J. A. at age 7. The head is in profile and turned to the right, an orientation that is typically seen in profiles by left-handed children. (This drawing is reproduced from *Young Children and Their Drawings,* by J. H. Di Leo. Brunner/Mazel, 1970.)
The word FATHER is now printed without the reversals that characterized her earlier attempts at writing.

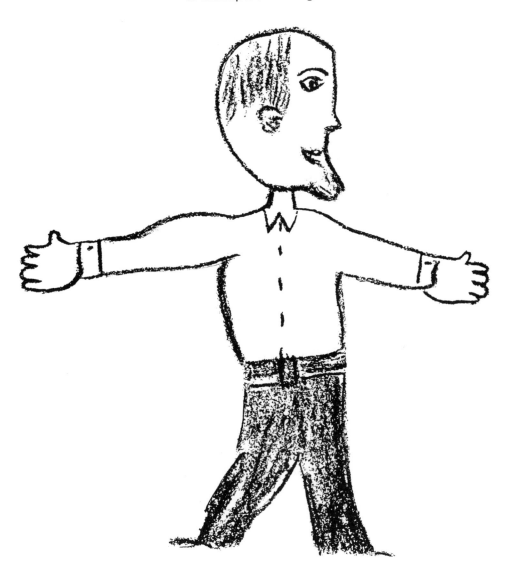

Reversal of letters and numbers

When the child whose drawings we have just seen (Figures 87 and 88) was in kindergarten, her first attempts at writing were characterized by reversal of many letters and numbers (Figures 89 and 90). This was a source of consternation to a well-intentioned but uninformed teacher who had to be reassured that it was not an indication of cerebral dysfunction. It is a frequent finding among left-handed children as they are learning to write. The teacher was advised against intervening. The child corrected her numbers and letters spontaneously in due course and, incidentally, went on to develop a most beautiful left-handed script.

Leonardo da Vinci wrote, painted, and drew with his left hand. Genius and consummate artist, he was able with unequalled mastery to portray the human form an infinite variety of postures and directional orientations. It is interesting to note, however, that in rapid sketching, his heads are predominantly turned to the right (Plate II).

Left-handed children, following their natural bent, will draw right-facing profiles.

Right-handed children may also have difficulty with left-right orientation when learning to write. Terry, a right-handed bright boy of 5 years 8 months, drew human figures on two successive days. In the first drawing, he printed his name from right to left reversing the letters (Figure 92). On the following day, he drew his mother and printed his name from left to right with letters in correct orientation (Figure 93). I was careful not to say anything that might have reflected on the reversals. Correction occurred spontaneously. Terry is not quite sure which direction his writing should take. He is an intelligent child with no signs whatever of brain dysfunction.

After all, reading and writing from left to right is no more natural than the other way round. It is a convention that must be taught and learned. The child learning Hebrew or Arabic must be taught to scan the page from right to left.

Various explanations have been offered to account for the fact that most children will draw a profile figure facing left. The left-to-right reading pattern has been mentioned. The need to see as one draws by not covering with the hand may be a factor. I am convinced that handedness is the prime determinant of profile orientation.

Directionality in drawing has been investigated widely here and abroad, notably by Gesell et al. (1974) and by Zazzo (1950).

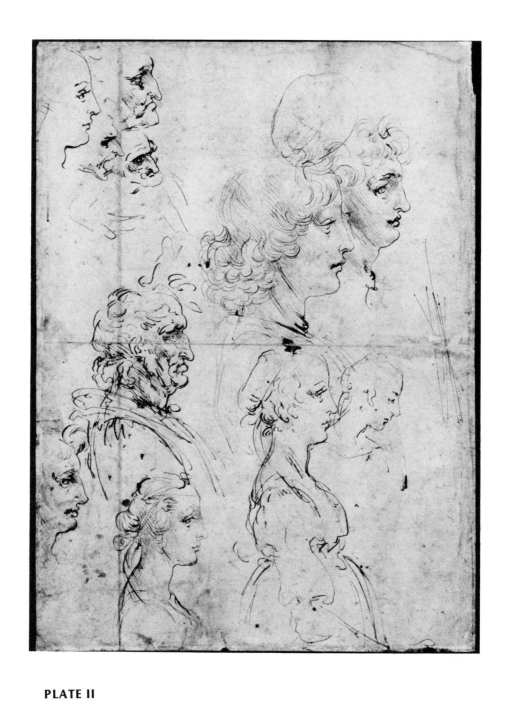

PLATE II

Leonardo da Vinci. Studies of heads. Royal Library, Windsor Castle. Copyright reserved.

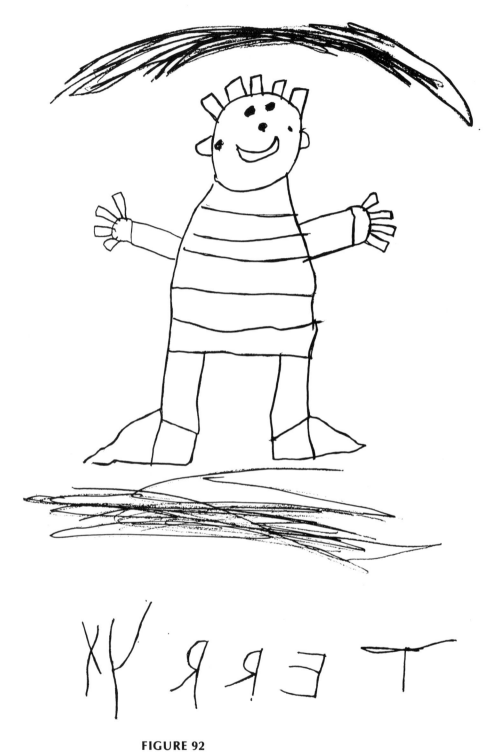

FIGURE 92

Drawn by Terry, age 5 years 8 months.

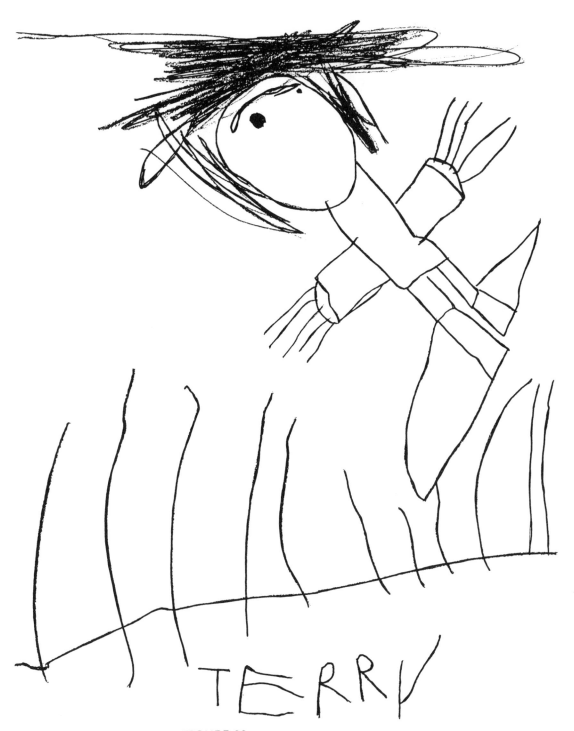

FIGURE 93

Drawn by Terry the following day.

Right-left

By age six, children are able to tell their right from their left hand. They may identify one or the other by the presence of a ring or a birthmark. But when asked to identify right or left of a person sitting opposite, they will point to the hand directly across their own right or left.

The ability to place oneself in the other's position — to "role play," as it were — does not emerge before 7 or 8 years of age. Prior to that time, children are quite egocentric and are unable to: master transformations; handle the variance between thought and image; or acquire concepts of conservation or reversibility. Things are taken at face value; the mirror image is not viewed as a reversal.

This same inability to tell right from left of a person sitting across is also shown when the child is presented with a picture of a person, even when the child has drawn the figure.

Visual realism does not usually appear in drawings until the artists are seven or eight years of age. They may then be ready to tell right and left in the picture of a person, as well as in the one facing or in their own mirror image.

Estimates as to the number of sinistrals among children vary between 5 and 10 percent, with a tendency towards the higher figure now that more children are spared the ill-advised intervention against their natural inclination to write with their left hand.

Cerebral dominance is undoubtedly at the bottom of hand preference, but there remains a possibility that outside influences may have been a factor in the enormous preponderance of right-handed persons. Evolution, natural selection, and prejudice against sinistrals have been invoked as contributory causes. This, of course, raises the long-interred spectrum of the inheritance of acquired characteristics, assuming that ambidextrality prevailed at the outset.

We are symmetrically constructed on the outside, but the inside is startlingly asymmetrical. Dextrocardia is a rare phenomenon; one can hardly conceive of that or other organ reversals as other than developmental aberrations that seriously impair their function. Such is not the case with sinistrality. Left-handed persons are not functionally impaired. There is no need to name the vast number of eminent persons who have excelled in various fields of human endeavor though sensing and approaching the world with left eye, hand, and foot. From Leonardo da Vinci to Charlie Chaplin, the roster is indeed impressive.

A survey of Eskimos reported by Dawson (1977) shows the incidence of left-handedness to be significantly higher than in other ethnic groups. The difference is related to permissive attitudes that prevail in the child-rearing practices of the Eskimo culture. Pressures for compliance are minimal and besides, handedness is not an issue in populations that subsist by hunting and fishing. The reported incidence of 11.3 percent for the Eskimos is in sharp contrast to the 1.5 percent reported in an agricultural Chinese population, in which pressures for conformity prevail.

Hemispheric specialization

At the level of the cerebral hemispheres, the human brain is asymmetrical in function as well as in structure. This duality, however, is far from absolute. Rather than a dominant hemisphere, it is more appropriate to speak of a predominant hemisphere, as suggested by Oppenheimer (1977). Hemispheric diversity has been clearly demonstrated for linguistic expression and spatial function.

The two sides of the brain do not function independently of each other; they are integrated structurally and functionally by the 200 million fibres of the corpus callosum and by the symmetrical, unifying structures of the subcortical system which radiate out into the lateralized hemispheres. Each side is complementary to the other.

Evidence for a split brain is derived from pathological, surgical, and electrical stimulating procedures. The results suggest the possibility of a split mind as well.

From a prognostic standpoint, it is heartening to know that since firm localization of function is not established in young children, damage to one or the other side of the brain does not result in permanent loss of speech or control as in adults or even in children over the age of five. Compensatory function by the intact hemisphere can be expected in the younger child.

Handedness and cognitive style

Cognitive style refers to the structure of thinking rather than to its content. The term is used to denote the way in which individuals conceptually organize and process information.

Evidence for the functional asymmetry of the human brain was firmly established during the nineteenth century with the pivotal discovery by Broca (1861) that a lesion of the third frontal convolution in the left hemisphere was associated with inability to articulate speech, though inner speech remained unaffected. But over and above this fact is the accumulating evidence that hemispheric specialization influences the way we interpret the environment—our cognitive style.

Evidence derived from patients who have undergone brain surgery indicates that the right hemisphere reasons in a holistic, intuitive manner and that it is specialized in spatial functions. The left hemisphere reasons in a predominantly analytical, logical style besides being specialized in linguistic skills.

Since handedness is governed by the contralateral hemisphere, it has been postulated that a relationship might be demonstrable between handedness and the cognitive style peculiar to the same side of the brain. Are left-handers more likely to reason holistically and respond intuitively, and are they better than right-handers in spatial functions? Are right-handers more logical and have they better language skills than their counterparts? Levy (1977) has been prominent in this line of investigation. He confirms the spatial specificity of the right or mute hemisphere and the linguistic specificity of the left or speaking hemisphere. He regards lateralization of function as exists in humans to be an evolutionary development not present in subhuman species and a major factor in the higher intellectual function that characterizes the human brain.

The functional asymmetry of the human brain vastly increases its cognitive potential. Reciprocal enrichment by each hemisphere's diverse activity promotes an integrated adaptive response.

Levy (1969) indicates that the advantage of functional lateralization is diminished when, as in left-handers, linguistic expression is shared by the right, ordinarily mute hemisphere, with resultant sacrifice of some of the specialized spatial function proper to the right hemisphere. Continuing investigation is directed at determining whether handedness implies a different cerebral organization.

Perception and cognitive style

One approach to the investigation of cognitive style is the assessment of field dependence/independence (Witkin et al., 1954). By their response to perceptual tasks, subjects are regarded as free or restricted in the way they organize and process information.

Rod-and-Frame (RFT) and Embedded Figures (EFT) tests are among the major tests devised for that purpose. Field-independent subjects are better at discriminating figure from background and at maintaining a perception of the vertical in the face of disorienting cues. Subjects who are field-dependent tend to be distracted from devoting selective attention in a context of irrelevant, compelling stimuli.

By influencing the way in which we perceive ourselves and the outer world, cognitive style expresses itself in social as well as in intellectual attitudes and behavior.

Cognitive style and body image in human figure drawings

Investigation of the ways in which we organize information has disclosed a relationship between cognitive style and personality. Field-dependence and field-independence are aspects of this relationship. Hypothesizing a comprehensive influence of perception on personality, Witkin and associates (1962) studied human figure drawings by young adults and school-age children. Their results indicate a connection between capacity to experience objects as discrete from their context and concept of body image as expressed in drawings.

The drawings were first rated according to a scale developed by Machover—basically a projective technique that referred directly to manifestations of anxiety and self-esteem. In addition, a scale developed by H. Marlens, a psychologist, was used to identify specific features leading to a global interpretation of the figure as primitive or sophisticated. In many respects, this scale based on observable items in the drawings is similar to the Goodenough-Harris Scale used to assess intellectual maturity.

As expected, the concept of body image assessed by these scales correlated positively with the level of field-independence as expressed in the RFT and EFT tests. The investigation supports the idea of consistency in the way we experience ourselves and the outer world.

Based on the contributions of anatomists, neurologists, psychiatrists, psychologists and other researchers and clinicians, the following connections may be viewed as a sequential chain:

1) Cerebral lateralization with tendency to perceive spatially, globally, and intuitively (right hemisphere); or analytically, logically, and articulately (left hemisphere), i.e., cognitive style.
2) Relationship between cognitive style and concept of self as well as of the world outside.
3) Concept of self in relation to the outer world as related to personality.
4) Body image as reflected in drawings is a useful medium for expression of personality.

Ultimately a relationship can be seen between structure and function—between cerebral lateralization and personality.

The inclination to perceive globally and intuitively rather than logically and analytically applies to the interpreter as well as to the subject. Both approaches contribute to a valid interpretation.

In summary, currently available evidence indicates:

1) Handedness is genetically influenced. It is an expression of brain lateralization.

2) Evidences of handedness are manifested in early infancy. It can be detected in the earliest scribbles as well as in the representational drawings of children.

3) An explanation is offered to account for the striking fact that the overwhelming majority of profiles face left.

4) As pressures to conform are relaxed, the incidence of left-handedness tends to increase.

5) Hemispheric specialization confers distinct advantages over the symmetric subhuman brain.

6) Though handedness and cognitive style are manifestations of hemispheric specialization, the relationship linking one with the other remains a question for ongoing study.

7) The role of perception in cognitive style is evident in the assessment of field-dependence/independence.

8) There is a positive relationship between body image as expressed in drawings and field-independence.

11

TREE DRAWINGS AND
PERSONALITY TRAITS

General considerations

Adolescents and adults may resist attempts to have them draw a person or they may comply with a summarily scribbled figure just to get it over with. Such a product can hardly be regarded as a representative specimen for diagnostic interpretation.

Faced with the problem of utter refusal or half-hearted compliance, the examiner will seek other ways. Among alternatives, the request to draw a tree may meet with a positive response denied the more obviously probing, personal draw-a-person situation. The armor of privacy, so dear to adolescents, remains apparently intact.

Based on the assumption that much of the personality is projected in the way a person draws a tree and its parts, a vast literature has emerged on the use and value of this test. In Europe, the Baumtest (Koch, 1949) is widely used, while in the USA tree drawing is an essential element of the House-Tree-Person Test (Buck, 1948). The psychological significance attributed by these authors to the omission or excessive emphasis on roots, trunk, and crown has not consistently been sustained by statistical analysis.

Muschoot and Demeyer (1974) embarked on a study aimed at reducing the subjective element inherent in interpretation. Theirs is a normative study of drawings by 200 girls and an equal number of boys at each level from age 5 to 17 years. This developmental approach reveals the usual and the deviant. Statistical analysis confirms many of the findings if not the significance of Koch's specific signs.

As is emphasized throughout this and in my earlier publications, a developmental perspective is essential if one is to avoid attributing deviance to omissions and peculiarities that are simply expressions of immaturity.

Symbolism of the whole and its parts

Hammer (1969), in comparing drawing of a person to drawing of a tree, finds a significant difference in the levels of personality opened up by the two techniques. He views the tree as tapping more basic, deeper layers of the personality, with an even deeper layer made accessible in the chromatic tree drawing. (He uses the term "achromatic" for a pencil drawing and "chromatic" for a colored crayon drawing.)

More recently, Bolander (1977) has contributed an impressive work in which every imaginable type and trait of tree are reproduced and analyzed for what they may express of the personality of the maker.

No attempt will be made to summarize these exhaustive works. Instead, some examples of tree drawings will be offered with brief comments. The reader is referred to the original studies by the authors cited in this introduction.

The projective use of tree drawings is based on the assumption that they are unconscious self-portraits. The three main regions of the tree are believed to represent the three major realms of the personality: the trunk—the emotional life; the roots—the instinctual; and the crown—the intellectual and social. These assumptions are supported by clinical evidence (e.g., Bolander, 1977, and Buck, 1974).

Tree drawings by children

Predominance of the emotional life is expressed by a large trunk in tree drawings by children. Along with persons, houses, animals, and suns, trees are frequently seen in children's spontaneous drawings. Typically, the trunk is emphasized up to about age seven (Piaget's preconceptual stage).

The interpretation generally given (Koch, Bolander) is that the trunk symbolizes the emotional realm and that since children during their earlier years are creatures of emotion, they project that aspect of their personality by emphasizing the trunk.

Figures 94 and 95 by young children show trunk emphasis. One child described as sociable has added persons and the sun. The other has also drawn the sun, but there is a darkened sky and no people; she is described as depressed. Figure 96 by a boy of 7 also shows a large trunk and a happy, shining sun.

FIGURE 94

By a girl, age 7. Trunk emphasis.

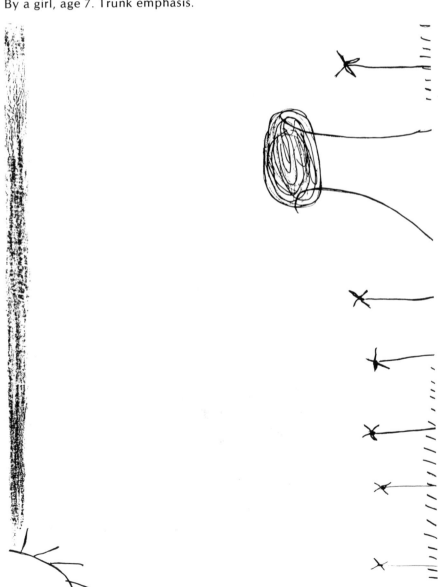

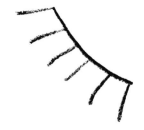

FIGURE 95

By Helen, age 6 years 6 months. Trunk emphasis.

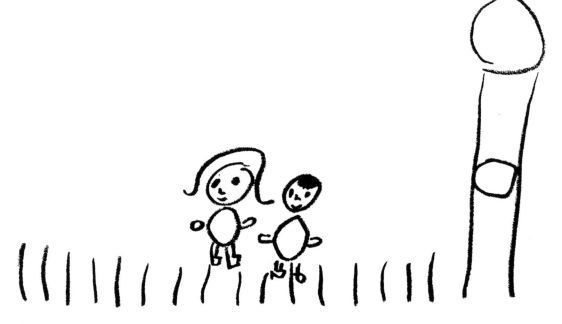

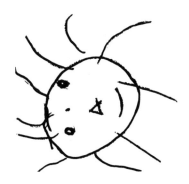

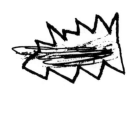

FIGURE 96
Drawn by a boy of 7 years.

FIGURE 97

By an unhappy, withdrawn boy of 10 years 11 months. Victim of a strife-ridden home. The tree is heavily shaded, cut off at top and bottom indicating repression of instinctual energy and social isolation (sealed-off crown). The large knot-hole suggests a traumatic event; the heavy shading, anxiety. The broad trunk express-es the intense emotional reaction to his plight. The apples may symbolize chil-dren (he retains a strong attachment to his many siblings).

According to Muschoot and Demeyer, fruit are most frequently seen at age 7. The fruit are typically unattached. By age 12, the fruit are generally attached by a stem, as in this drawing. Beyond age 14, the presence of fruit is regarded as an in-dication of childishness.

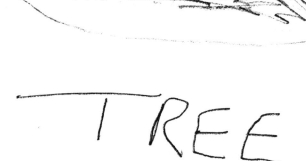

Animals in knotholes

This amusing feature occurs in outdoor scenes by school-age chil-dren.

Figure 98 by a girl of 10 years and 10 months is described by her as depicting a bunny in his home. Figure 99 by a girl of 12 shows a squirrel.

Both girls live at home with their parents. The younger attends fifth grade; the other is in seventh grade. Both are prepubertal. They appear well-adjusted. There are no unusual difficulties in their behav-ior at home or in school. Both drawings were made spontaneously.

In preadolescent children, I can see no significance in this feature other than the expression of a vivid fantasy.

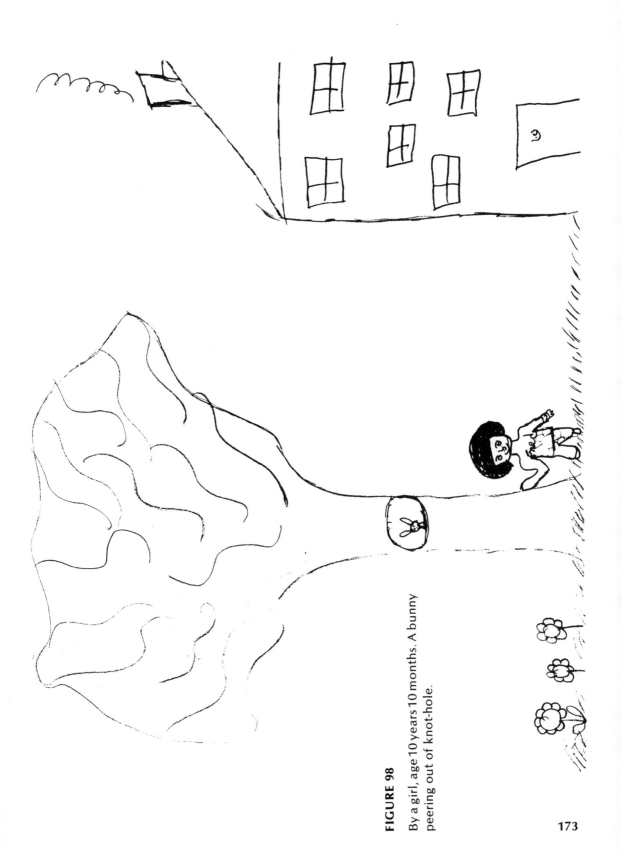

FIGURE 98

By a girl, age 10 years 10 months. A bunny peering out of knot-hole.

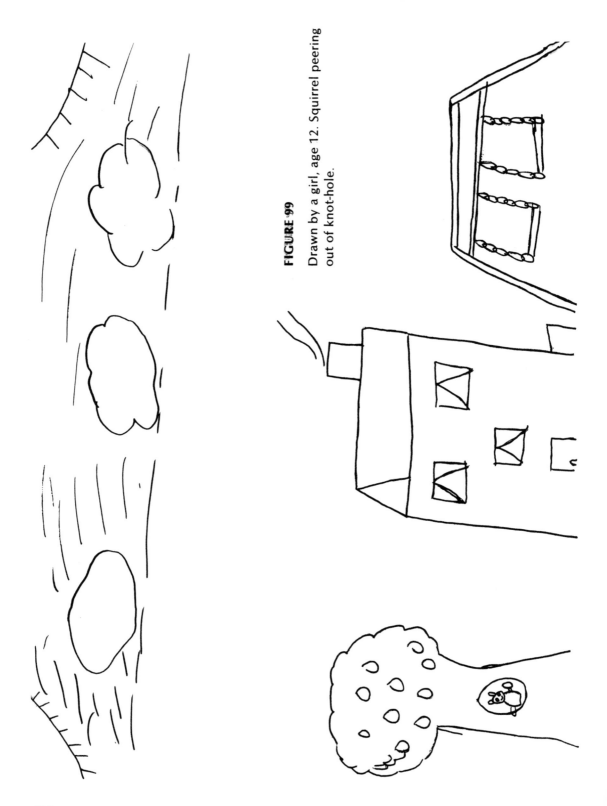

FIGURE 99

Drawn by a girl, age 12. Squirrel peering out of knot-hole.

12

EMOTIONAL DISORDER REFLECTED IN DRAWINGS

Drawings by persons relatively free of cultural restraints

There are among us three groups whose art may be regarded as genuine and authentic because it is largely, if not totally, free from cultural intrusion:

1) young children, still clinging to a vision as seen by the innocent eye;
2) the mentally subnormal, who are incapable of assimilating the culture;
3) those we call mad, because they resist or reject our reality. (The art of this last group may be the purest form of self-expression.)

Mind and feelings are projected more genuinely when outside influences do not impose conformism. Free from cultural restraints, drawings more validly express their makers' individuality and are of special interest to the diagnostician and therapist.

In common, the artwork of the three groups tells more about the artists themselves than about the object portrayed. But there the similarity ends. Oversimplification tends to lump the three together, but such a view is fallacious. The retarded 10-year-old who is functioning at a 5-year-old level is not the same as the normal 5-year-old either in mentation or in personality. The regressed adult behaving childishly is not the same as a child behaving at age level. If the makers of art are so different, how can their art express anything more than an illusory similarity?

On a quantitative scale, the three may attain the same score, but differences emerge when the quality of their product is considered.

Drawings by retarded children

Figure 100 by a retarded child of 7 years reveals a total lack of foresight and planning. Only one hand can be fitted into the available space. He has drawn the hand with supernumerary fingers, while neglecting those parts that come to mind earlier to normal children, namely, the mouth, hair, and feet.

FIGURE 100

Drawn by a mentally retarded boy of 7 years. Treatment for phenylketonuria was started late, at age 29 months. The condition was detected only after it was found in a younger sibling.

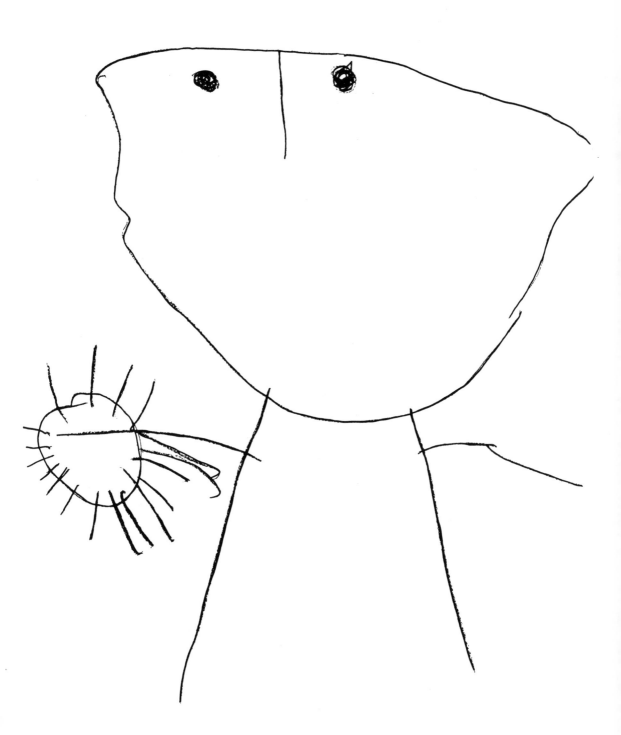

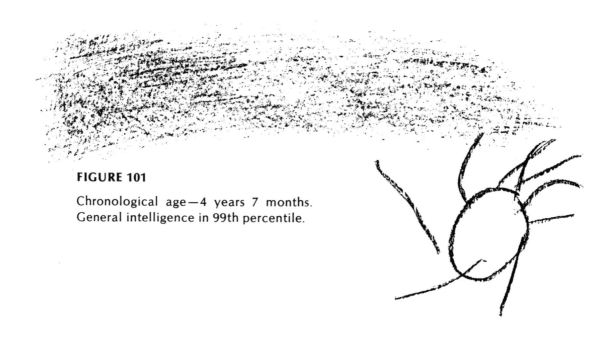

FIGURE 101

Chronological age—4 years 7 months.
General intelligence in 99th percentile.

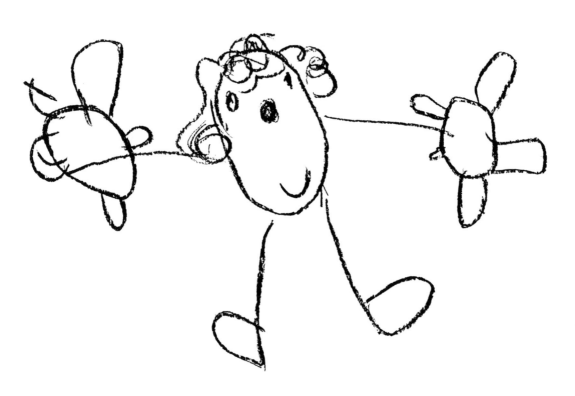

On a quantitative scale, the drawing expresses a mental age of 4 years 9 months. In essence, the drawing is quite different from that of a normal child of that chronological age. Figure 101 is by a normal child of 4 years 7 months. The difference is essentially qualitative. The normal child of seven does not paint himself into a corner as does this retarded child, who begins to draw without prior consideration of how the figure will relate to the environment as represented by the sheet of paper on which he is about to draw.

The retarded child is not like a younger child; the difference is not only of degree but of kind as well. Qualitative differences are real and substantial despite their resistance to numerical expression. Perhaps everything cannot be measured. Be that as it may, in the present state of the art, a holistic approach is more productive of valid information than the atomistic, item by item appraisal.

Drawings by emotionally disturbed children

In viewing Figure 102 by a boy of 7 years 7 months, one is impressed by the expression of fear conveyed by the raised eyebrows and narrowed rectangular mouth and then by the selection of the backbone as a prominent element in rendering the body image. In my interview of the child and parents, I was unable to unearth any reason for this unusual interest in the spinal column. There was no case of spina bifida nor any record of a visit to the chiropractor.

In this drawing it is the quality of the drawing and not the number of parts that makes it different from drawings by other children of the same age. The child was emotionally disturbed. He had been hospitalized for a month for treatment of anorexia. (The facial expression reminds me of Edvard Munch's terrifying image of fear "The Scream.")

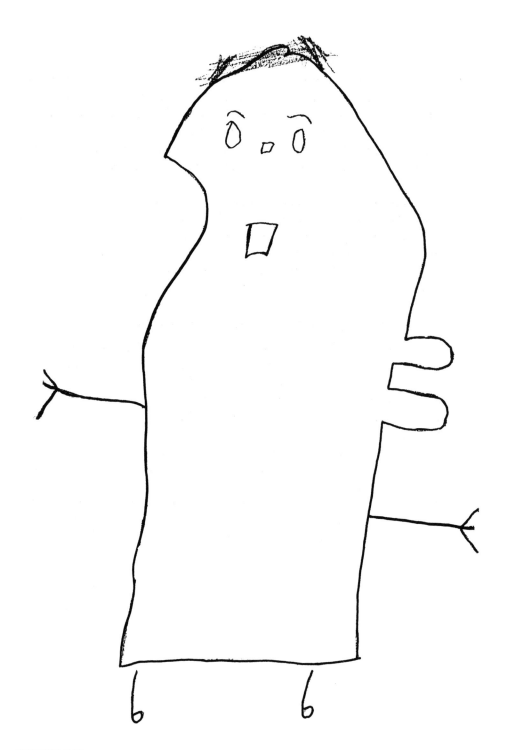

FIGURE 102

By a boy of 7 years 7 months. Hospitalized for treatment of anorexia.

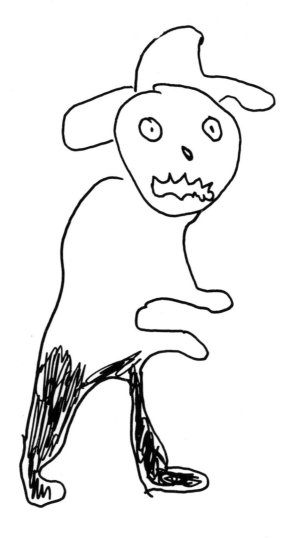

FIGURE 103

Figure drawing at age 7 years 9 months.
Note the fierce expression. Teacher thinks
the boy is mad at the world.

The three drawings that follow (Figures 104, 105 and 106) are by a boy from a broken home. He is receiving therapy in a residential treatment center. The drawings made at intervals of time show an unusual recurrent theme described by him as his parents throwing "something" into the garbage pail.

The child's psychiatrist believes that "something" to symbolize his feelings of rejection—that he is the object being discarded. Recurrence of the theme shows how deeply the feeling is impressed in the boy's psyche. The drawings were made at 7 years 1 month, 7 years 4 months, and 8 years of age.

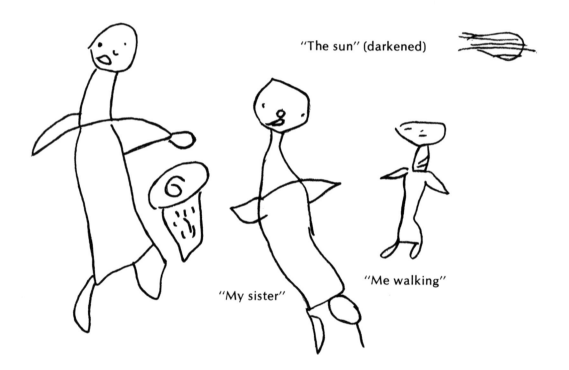

"The sun" (darkened)

"My sister"

"Me walking"

FIGURE 104

K-F-D drawn by R.B., a boy age 7 years 1 month.
"My mother throwing something in the garbage"
Examiner: "What is she throwing?"
Child: (hesitates) "Paper."

182

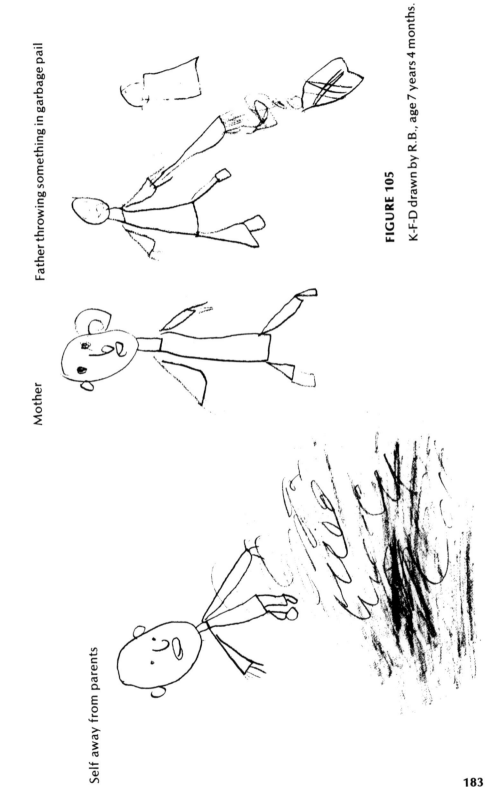

Father throwing something in garbage pail

Mother

Self away from parents

FIGURE 105

K-F-D drawn by R.B., age 7 years 4 months.

183

Mother throwing something in garbage pail

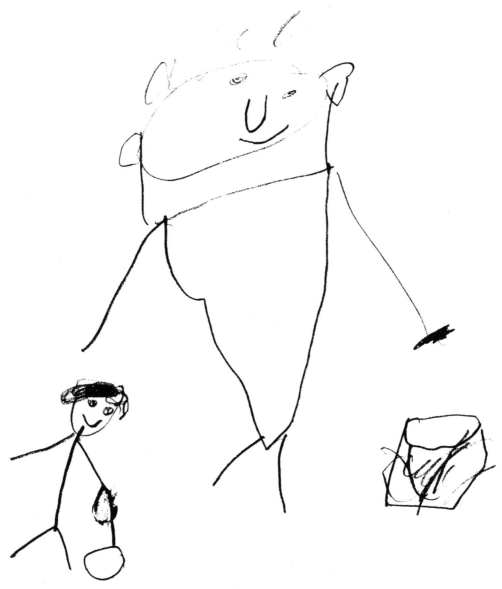

Sister playing with yo-yo

FIGURE 106

K-F-D drawn by R.B., age 8 years.

Eros and Thanatos

The three drawings that follow (Figures 107, 108 and 109) are by a boy of 9 years 9 months. There is a prevailing atmosphere of high tension in the home. Male violence and female acquiescence alternate with overt sexual activity between the parents.

His drawings reveal his perception of the sex roles and his own re-action to the unfortunate situation. In the self-portrait, facial expression conveys his anger; emphasis on teeth, aggression; and huge ears, ideas of reference. The overall impression is hostility.

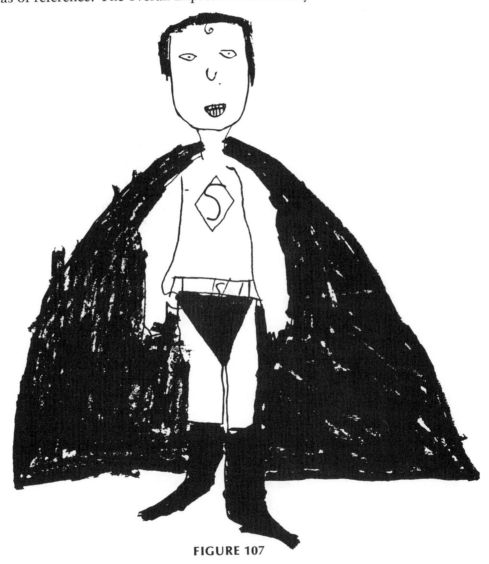

FIGURE 107

Drawn by a boy, age 9 years 9 months.
Power.

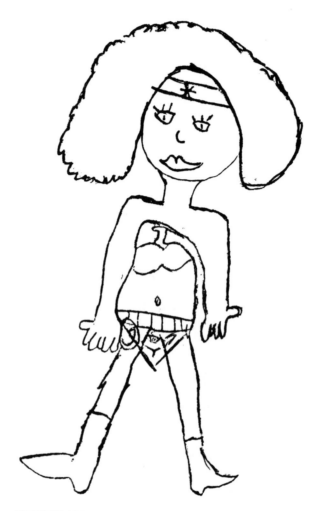

FIGURE 108

Drawn by a boy, age 9 years 9 months.
Seduction

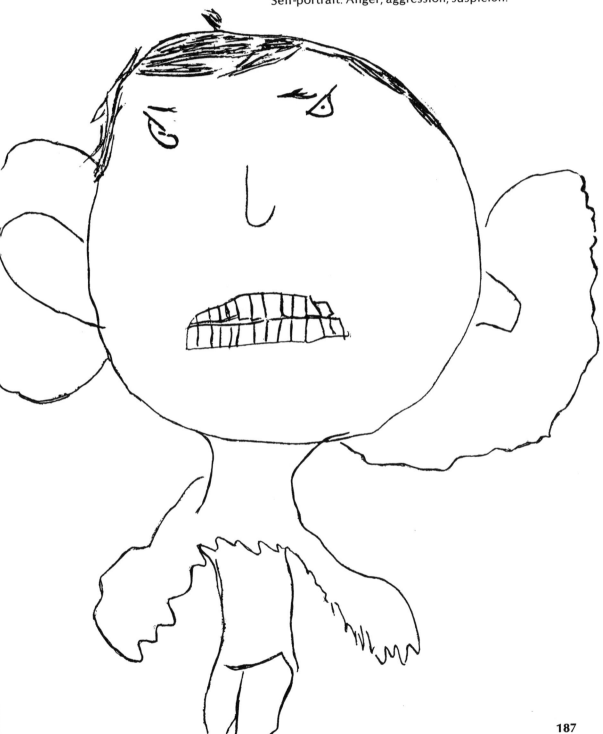

FIGURE 109

Drawn by a boy, age 9 years 9 months.
Self-portrait. Anger, aggression, suspicion.

Creativity — madness — child art

Individuals endowed with unusual imaginative insight and intuitive perception find themselves separated from the society of their time. Such is the fate of those who would push beyond the boundaries of cultural equilibrium. History is replete with those who were regarded as eccentric, maladjusted, or dangerous, only to be extolled by future generations. Socrates, Leonardo da Vinci, Galileo, and in our time, Van Gogh, are recipients of belated appreciation.

Genius expressed in the realm of science or art continues to challenge understanding. It has been related to madness, since those outside the culture must be mad (sic)! The case of Van Gogh would seem to support such a view, as some of his finest work coincided with his progressive deterioration. During his final period at Auvers, his paintings strikingly reflected intense emotion and overwhelming melancholy. His last work, prophetically portrayed an ominous flight of crows across a dark, turbulent sky over a storm-tossed cornfield. Having completed this violent, gloomy scene, he shot himself.

Freud tried to explain Leonardo da Vinci and his art by psychoanalysis. Herbert Read considered the essential elements of art to be irrational and intuitive; he saw the artist in a creative phase as bringing to the surface material from a cauldron of timeless, intensively vital entities. During that moment, the artist would be free from restrictions of ego, superego, and culture — an interpretation that is more fitting to those artists who work rapidly, in a state of tension. Van Gogh is an excellent example of this type of artist. He painted directly and abundantly: 800 paintings and 900 drawings all in the space of his last 10 years. Even his landscapes turned into self-portraits in which the viewer experiences the heightened emotional temperature of the time the work was being made.

In contrast, there is Leonardo working slowly and only after numerous sketches before taking up the brush. He took three years to do "The Last Supper," unperturbed by the dismay and protestations of the monks who had commissioned the work. Whatever reservations one may have regarding Freud's analysis of Leonardo, it is clear from that study and from every biography past and current, that this extraordinary, gifted, artist-scientist was a reflective and not an impulsive person — one who produced a dozen paintings in a long life, most of them unfinished. At no time did he drop his intellectual guard and allow emotion full sway. Even the sexual act is viewed with cool detachment as a trap laid to ensnare by pretty faces and sensual natures.

Psychologist Frank Barron, in his study of the personality of creative people from various fields, used the Minnesota Multiphasic Personality Inventory to show that creative persons ranked with schizophrenics on the Schizophrenia Scale but differed sharply and significantly on the Ego Strength Scale in which the schizophrenics did poorly. In the light of these findings, it was inferred that the two groups, the creatively successful individuals and the psychotic, differed on one crucial factor: in the former, madness was controlled.

Because it too is free from cultural restraints, the art of young children has been compared to that of the alienated adult. The similarities have been attributed to predominance of instinctual and emotional forces. The comparison is misleading. True, fantasy life is vivid in both groups; but, as will be shown later in this work, similarities appear only when the adult psychotic is in a regressive phase. As the psychosis becomes more stabilized, the artwork is strikingly and substantially different from anything made by young children.

Regressive drawings compared with immature drawings of normal children

During the early stages of schizophrenic conflict or during phases of regression, drawings may superficially resemble those by young children. Careful examination, however, will reveal the similarities to be illusory. At first glance, and without prior information, one may at times be misled into attributing to a child the drawing by a psychotic adult. This is not surprising if one considers that in both, primary thought process prevails. In both psychotic person and preoperational child the view is highly subjective, dominated by feelings, imbued with fantasy, and largely free from cultural and logical restraints. As a result, human figure drawings are typically schematic, reduced to what the maker regards as essential. Body proportions are unrealistic, with what is thought important expressed disproportionately large, and complete disregard of linear perspective. If drawn by an adult, one is likely to call the figure "bizarre." Drawn by a child, the figure is "wrong" by adult standards. What many conventional adults fail to appreciate is that the pre-latency child, as well as the alienated adult, is telling more about the self than about the object drawn.

In the young child, such peculiarities express a developmental stage. Corresponding to each stage in cognitive growth is a specific system of figuration (Di Leo, 1970, 1977). In the mentally ill, similar characteristics express a striving to represent vision, thought, and feelings of a personality that is attempting to reduce the intolerable, frightening influx of impressions from without.

A prerequisite for valid interpretation is a developmental perspective. What is normal at one age may reveal serious pathology at another. The normal child, in maturing towards latency, progresses from primary to secondary thought process, from irrationality to logic, from egocentricity to objectivity, from pleasure to reality principle. Creative minds may have unusual accessibility to primary process but secondary thought process remains in control (Arieti, 1976).

Art Brut

As the schizophrenic process advances and psychotic structures become stabilized, secondary conscious process intervenes, giving rise to a form of art peculiar to the psychotic. It has no counterpart in art sanctioned by the culture and displayed for admiration by the public in museums and galleries. The makers of this "outsider art" are supremely individualistic and nonconformist. Jean Dubuffet calls it "Art Brut" and regards it as a genuine expression of greater merit than the art we have been conditioned to respect.

Though each maker is mad in a very personal way, there are features that express a common underlying striving to create a world in which one can find the balance, order, and stability that elude the person in objective reality. Sanity might be the madness that the schizophrenic rejects. Be that as it may, art work in the later stages of psychosis tends to resemble the intricate, symmetrical, elaborate patterning of those Persian rugs with their profusion of formal elements, geometric figures, repeated again and again, and meticulously reproduced in the corresponding half of the composition. Is it a fanatical preoccupation with symmetry? Or is it a retreat from the intolerable chaos of a bewildering world?

Frequently observed in Art Brut is the apparent need to fill every available area with small figures, creating an excessively crowded effect suggesting fear of open spaces.

Art Brut bears no similarity to the art of children, nor to the art of those who were artists before they became mentally ill. It is raw art in a class by itself. Secondary process intrudes but fails to control the fantasy and irrationality emanating from the deepest layer of the personality.

The art of the mentally ill has an abiding fascination for mental health professionals. Their attempts to relate stylistic features to specific forms of mental illness have been rejected as worthless not only by many of their colleagues but by artists who have been attracted to the art work by persons diagnosed as psychotic. Jean Dubuffet is outspoken in his resistance to the very notion of an art of the insane. Thévoz (1976) denies any diagnostic value to the art work of the mentally ill, claiming that according to the criteria used by early twentieth century psychiatrists Picasso, Ernst, and Klee could manifest a variety of pathology.

There is no denying that the art in question reveals unusually vivid imagination and fantasy. Despite Dubuffet's statement that there is no art of madness any more than there is an art of people with knee trouble, he has been a collector and ardent champion of the art of the alienated. It is different from the art of those who are able to control their fantasies. The differences remain a fertile field for study. A global view must, however, also take into account the opinions of those who are gifted with unusual insight into a visionary world.

A striking characteristic of drawings by young children is reduction of the human figure to its essentials: head, eyes, mouth, nose, arms and legs. Despite the simplicity of the drawing, the viewer is fully aware that the schema represents a person.

Similar stripping to essentials is observed in drawings by psychotic individuals who represent the human figure impoverished and devoid of any elements of feeling. As mentioned earlier, the developmental lack of skill and maturity of the young child cannot be identified with the withdrawal from reality of the psychotic individual. Though the drawings may be strikingly similar, psychologically the two expressions are worlds apart.

As the schizophrenic person learns to live with his process, artistic expression assumes a form that is peculiar to his nosological group. Patterns of elaborate design, strictly formalized, symmetrical, replete with ornamental features suggest a visionary world fully under the artist's control. Examination of the work will reveal the symbolic nature of the tiny elements that fill the composition as related to events in the artist's early life. This type of art has no counterpart in the art of children; nor for that matter, in that of persons who are reacting meaningfully to the real world.

To illustrate what has been referred to as the purest expression of individuality, I have selected drawings by a psychotic artist who, without prior training, began to draw in a most remarkable way at age 35 and produced an enormous quantity of work during 35 years of confinement in a mental institution.

The confluence of negative familial and biological influences, deprivation, neglect, and the sequence of guilt and insanity with the eventual relief from torment in artistic expression are nowhere so strikingly proclaimed than in the detailed life history of Adolf Wölfli, the self-styled St. Adolf II, Captain of the Almighty-Giant-Steamship. (In real life, he worked as farm laborer, handyman, migrant worker; later, during his internment, he became a writer, draughtsman, artist, composer.)

Receiving only mere basic, oft-interrupted elementary education, forced to earn his keep by menial labor while but a child, neglected and abandoned, shifted from one foster home to another, strongly attached to an unrealistic image of a good, loving mother, Wölfli, despite all this, has produced a prodigious volume of drawings that attract the admiring attention of the art world.

The miseries of childhood were intensified by feelings of guilt occasioned by the sex urges of adolescence. An intense depression followed a love affair abruptly terminated by the girl's parents. Progressive psychological deterioration is evidenced by a sequence of sexual assaults on female children — a child of 14, then one of 7 — for which he spent two years in detention, eventually culminating in sexual abuse of a child of 3 which led to his confinement in an asylum for the mentally ill. There he spent the rest of his 35 years, dying of cancer at age 66.

It is during these years at the Waldau clinic that he begins to draw vividly, consuming innumerable pencils in the production of material that reaches a piled height of 2 meters. He jealously stores his work to which he attaches fantastic monetary value. At his death, he has not completed his Funeral March.

It is not the formidable quantity but the artistic level and psychological meaning of his prodigious work that provide fascinating material for study of the relationship of art to mental illness: the surfacing of images from the deepest recesses of the psyche and the cathartic and therapeutic effect resulting from the liberation of repressed, unconscious tormenting forces. On the back of the drawings there is often a carefully written explanation in which he may attribute the product to divine inspiration.

Artists, psychiatrists, and writers have examined the phenomenon of Adolf Wölfli. Exhibits of his work have been on display in art galleries all over Europe and in some American cities.

Plate III will give some idea of the throbbing imagination, symbolism, preoccupation with symmetry, and what Morgenthaler, his psychiatrist, calls "horror vacui" which cause the artist to fill each space with tiny "vögeli" and other obsessively repeated stereotyped motifs. ("Vögeli" are the little birds with human faces and wings.)

Can schizophrenic subtypes be distinguished by their drawings?

Even without prior information, human figure drawings may permit differentiation between those by psychotic and nonpsychotic persons. Beyond these two divergent categories, some clinicians have noted features that distinguish schizophrenic subtypes. Kay (1978) reported significant differences in human figures drawn by retarded and non-retarded schizophrenic patients. The retarded manifested their intellectual subnormality by omission of details and errors of size and placement. Drawings by the non-retarded patients were more likely to express abnormality rather than deficit. Among the non-retarded

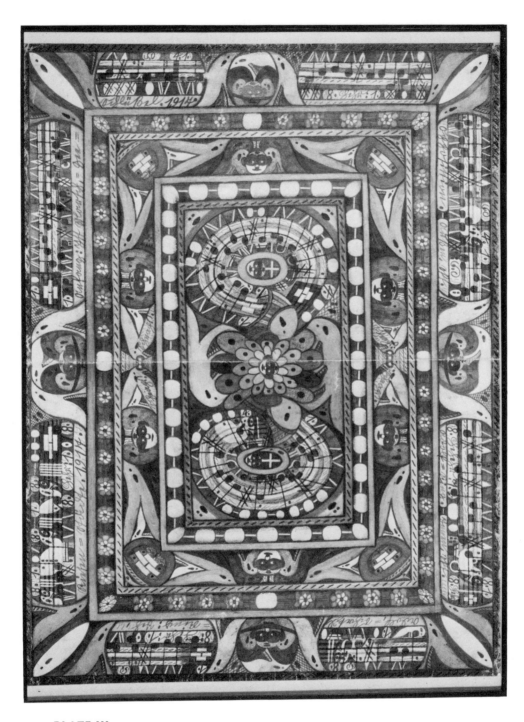

PLATE III

Adolf Wölfli. Riesen-Stadt, Waaben-Hall. 1917. Inv. 1964.80. Kunstmuseum Basel, Kupferstichkabinett.

schizophrenic subjects, drawings by the paranoid showed greater bizarreness. This is not surprising in view of the prevalence of delusions in the group. Interestingly, the earlier stages of schizophrenia showed perceptual confusion in the frequent appearance of inanimate figures when the subject was requested to draw a person. These findings will, no doubt, stimulate further study along these lines. The differences noted are all based on a global view of the drawings, not on specific details.

13

PITFALLS

Inconsistency in drawing performance

A bright girl, age 6 years 2 months, has drawn her mother (Figure 110). Mother has no teeth. She then draws her father (Figure 111). Father has teeth. One might conclude that the child perceives father as more aggressive, since teeth are believed to be symbolic of that trait.

But later on, that same day, the child draws another image (Figure 112), which she calls mother. Aside from other differences from the original figure (long, straight hair, eyelashes on both, neck) this one, in contrast to the other, has prominent teeth like father. It is this inconsistency that should be taken into account, especially in drawings by children.

Those features that appear consistently have been integrated into the child's concept. Other features that do not appear consistently are those in process of integration. This pitfall in interpretation can be avoided by withholding conclusions until several specimens have been examined, a precaution to be kept in mind with young children.

Mother is MIM

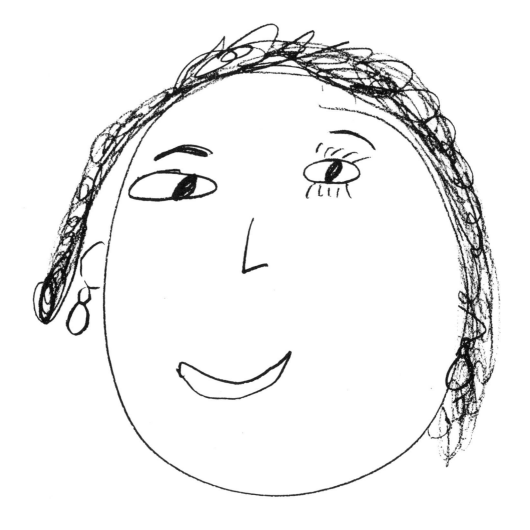

FIGURE 110

Drawn by a girl, age 6 years 2 months.

Father is

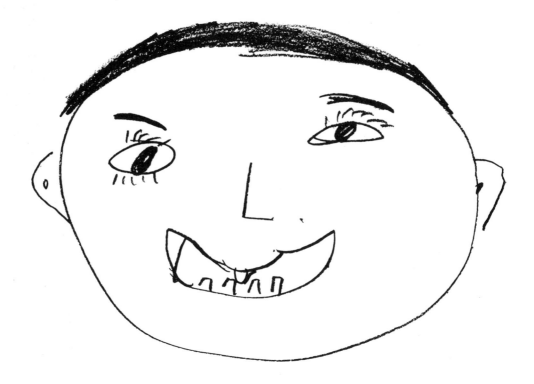

FIGURE 111

Drawn by a girl, age 6 years 2 months.

FIGURE 112

"Mother" drawn by a girl, age 6 years 2
months.

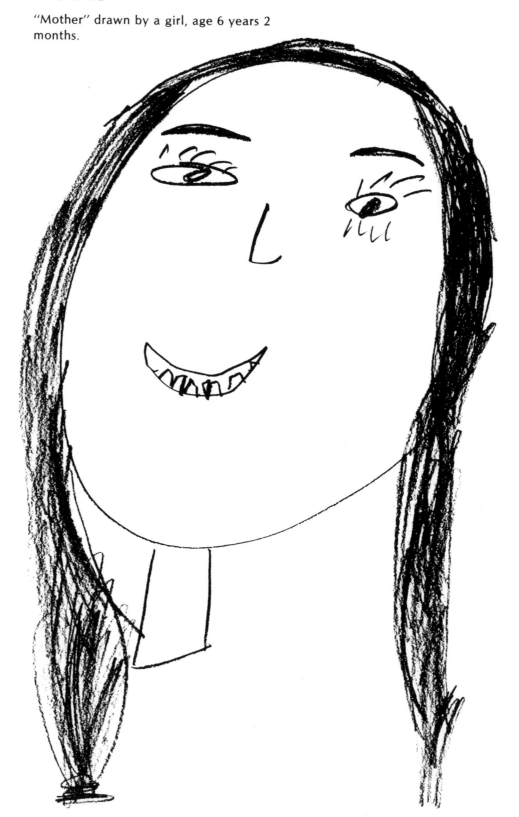

Excessive weight attached to details

How one may be misled by focusing on detail has been discussed in Chapter 7. It may suffice here to repeat that a detail assumes more significance when there are others pointing in the same direction and when the specific detail is concordant with the holistic impression derived from the drawing.

Failure to appreciate environmental factors

Will, age 10 years 2 months, was asked to draw a tree. He drew a Christmas tree (Figure 113). Stuart, age 11 years 5 months, was asked to draw a tree. He, too, drew a Christmas tree (Figure 114). But there's a significant difference. Will drew his on December 23. Stuart drew his on April 30.

Clearly, Will was influenced by the impending feast day, while Stuart drew his out of season. It is quite plausible to infer that while Will is simply responding to the joyous holiday spirit, Stuart is expressing a yearning or, let us say, a remembrance of things past.

Another example of the importance of outside factors is offered in Chapter 11. A barren tree drawn in winter is significantly and symbolically different from a barren tree drawn in summer.

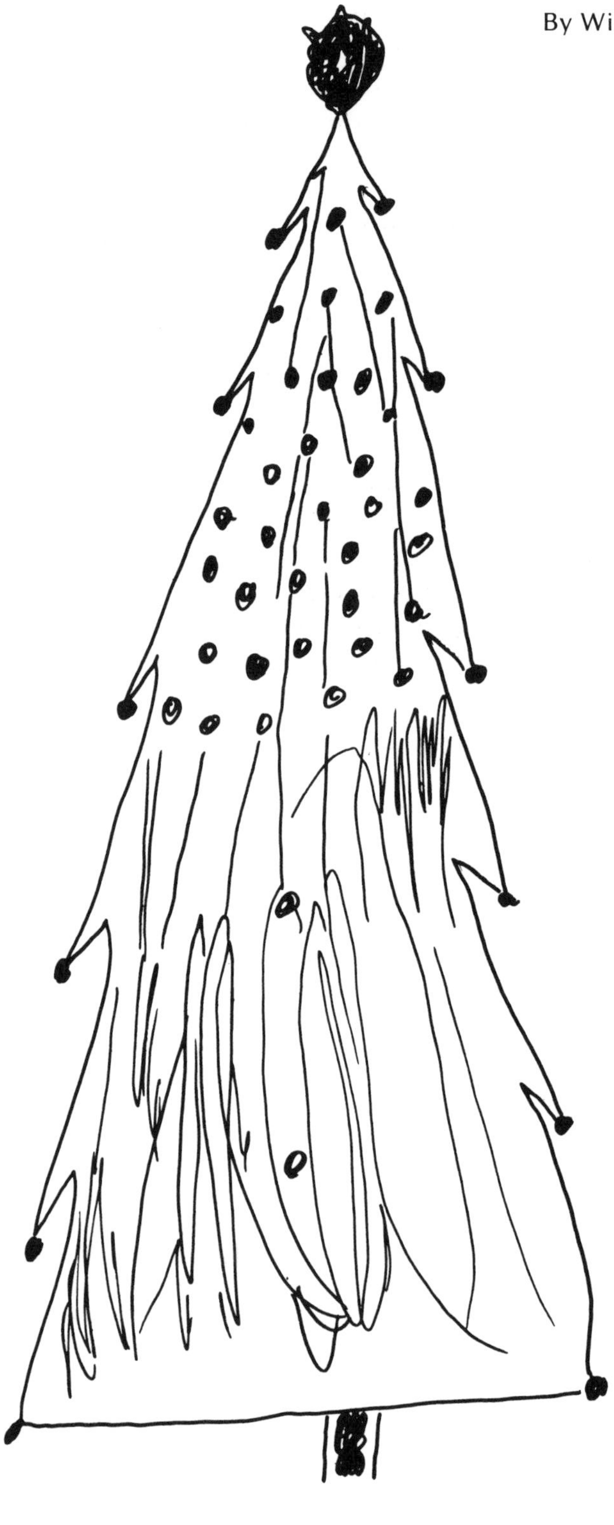

FIGURE 113

By Will, on December 23.

FIGURE 114

By Stuart, on April 30.

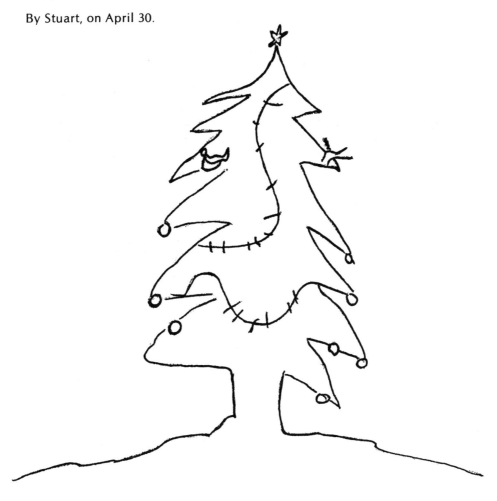

Excessive reliance on drawings in diagnosis

In the assessment of intellect and personality, drawings play a prominent role, often an indispensable one, particularly where verbal communication is impaired or repressed. At times, the drawing may tell so clearly as to render superfluous the need for other, supporting evidence. While such may be true in some instances, prudence reminds us that drawings should always be regarded as but one item in a comprehensive evaluative procedure. The contribution made by drawings varies from person to person; it may be strikingly revealing, vague, or contradictory.

There is general agreement that seriously disturbed children produce drawings that show the human figure as "bizarre" (for want of a better term), barely recognizable, poorly integrated, often with body parts scattered, lacking integration. Figure 115 is just such a drawing. It is quite different from those of other children the same age. Elaine, age 4 years 8 months, has drawn a person with the number of parts expected of children her age. Developmental evaluation confirms the impression of fully average mentation as derived from the Goodenough-Harris appraisal of her drawing. The scatter of body parts, however, suggests a lack of integration of personality. The impression conveyed by the drawing is at variance with her behavior, which is described as that of a sociable, secure, communicative child. Abnormal is the drawing, not the child.

Failure to combine the parts into an integrated whole is of pathological significance when it occurs beyond the preschool years.

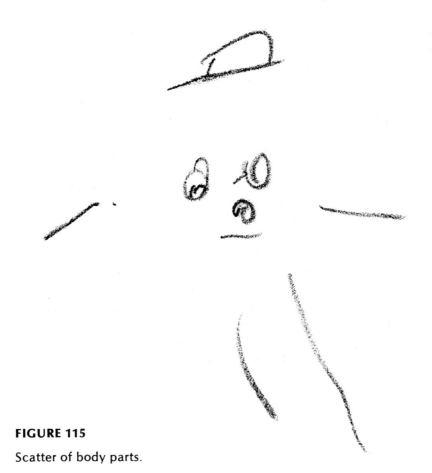

FIGURE 115

Scatter of body parts.

Ubiquitous sexual symbols

The infinite number and variety of sexual symbols derived from dreams and represented in art tends to obscure other material that may be of major significance to the individual concerned.

One can hardly draw any subject without allegedly phallic or female symbols. Sticks, umbrellas, knives, guns, aeroplanes, fishes, serpents, even the hand and foot have their counterparts in caves, boxes, ships, houses, rooms, stoves, even paper and books. The very ubiquity of these objects in the environment and in drawings leads to overwhelming confusion if one is to focus on symbols, forgetting the personality who related the dream or made the drawing.

There is no denying the significance of many objects and actions as expressions of the unconscious mental life. But in viewing the work of children, their vivid imagination and the tendency of some to elaborate may account for inclusion of numerous items whose symbolism may not be as clearly sexual as it would be if the drawing were by adolescents or adults.

As an example, take this drawing (Figure 116) by Patricia, a bright girl of 10. Is the child giving expression to a vivid imagination or is she struggling to keep afloat in a sea of phallic symbols (fishes, periscope)? She is prepubertal, of latency age, doing well in fourth grade, and presenting no unusual problems. There is a strong temptation to interpret the drawing in psychoanalytic terms—possibly, it is an unconscious expression of threats still in the offing. The drawing, however, should not be taken in isolation. It should be related to her present and future behavior, and to her personal history.

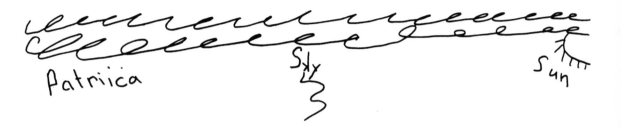

FIGURE 116

By Patricia, age 10.

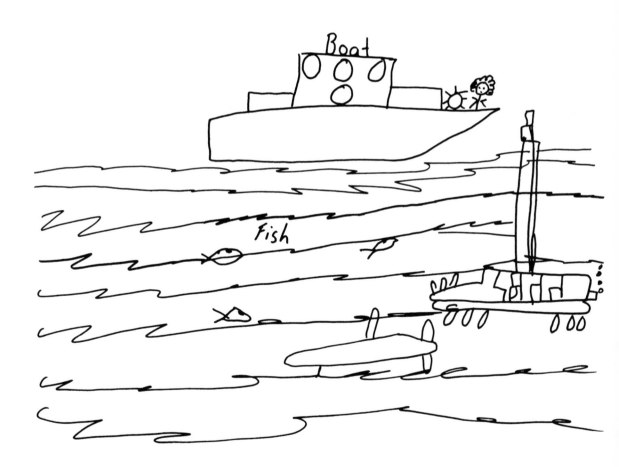

FIGURE 117

Despite its form, I do not believe the figure to be a phallic symbol. The artist is a child of 2 years 9 months. She told me it is a boat with a sail and I believe her.

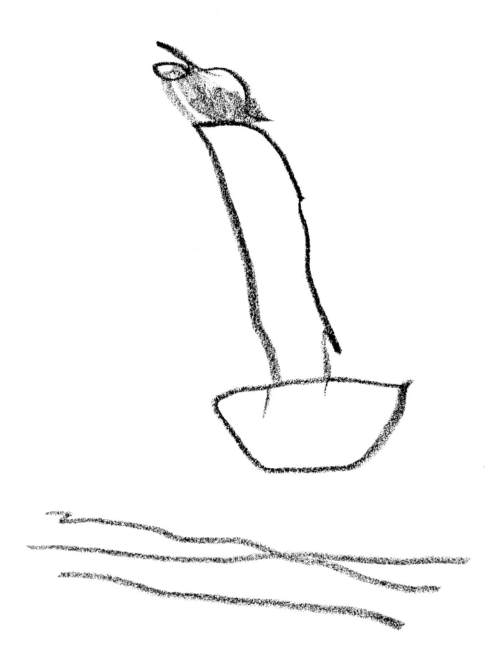

Mechanistic, point-by-point interpretation

Such a simplistic procedure may be carried to the extreme in which a checklist may be processed impersonally. Head, eyes, nose, mouth, arms, genitalia are among the highly significant symbolic elements in a drawing, particularly as they are emphasized, reduced, or omitted. This is also true of the formal and structural aspects of the figures, such as size, stance, shading, quality of line, placement in a group. A mechanistic approach can only lead to error. Valid interpretation cannot be achieved unless the projected material is related to the person who made it and unless product and producer are evaluated by a competent examiner.

A holistic approach that comprises the items and considers their relationship to each other and to the global theme is more productive diagnostically. What is the first impression conveyed by the whole scene? How does it look after the various items have been identified? Do the two perceptions coincide?

The interpretation of symbols cannot be governed by hard-and-fast rules. A symbol may be universal, but its meaning is individual. Drawings may provide new insights; they may confirm what we already know. Taken out of context, they may mislead.

14

THE ROLE OF THE ARTS IN EDUCATION FOR PEACE

The arts speak a universal language

"Without art, visual, verbal and musical,
our world would have remained a jungle."
Bernard Berenson

Amid so many forces that exert a negative, divisive, degrading pull on mankind, the arts emerge as a refuge and a hope. Free from limitations of time and space, the arts speak a universal language, communicating thoughts and feelings above and beyond the basic strivings of our animal nature.

The visual arts, music, dance, and the spoken and written arts by their universal appeal contribute toward tearing down the artificial barriers that separate human beings from each other.

The uniqueness of the visual arts

While the common effect of the arts is to cultivate and elevate, the individual arts do not accomplish this effect in the same way.

Music, the dance, the theatre, and literature convey their message over a period of time, so that meaning is dependent upon a memory of what has gone before, while the visual arts offer their conceptual and emotional content at once. Color, form, spatial relationships, and content are presented simultaneously without the need for prior sequences to impart meaning to the action under immediate consideration, as is essential to the other forms of artistic expression.

Of all the arts, music alone has the power to stir the emotions to an intense and immediate pitch. Literature, as in Dante's tale of Paolo and Francesca, may stir emotions and desires and influence thought, but its action is necessarily discursive and not immediate enough to tingle the spine on presentation. The dance, too, may bring a tear at the tragic fate of the star-crossed youthful lovers, but this final effect can only result from an awareness of what has gone before.

Music and the visual arts

But there is yet another striking difference between music and the visual arts.

There are numerous, well-documented cases in which children have displayed an impressive ability not only to perform, but even to compose music. Mozart is the best known of these gifted individuals.

In the visual arts, however, no such phenomenon can be identified with any degree of certainty. True, there are tales of remarkable talent manifested in childhood by Giotto, Cimabue, and others. But where are these manifestations of budding genius? There is every reason to believe that such stories are invented by effusive biographers. There is not a single work of artistic merit that has been drawn, painted, or modeled by a child, comparable to what children have achieved as musicians, composers, or directors of orchestras. Granted that there is a significant difference, to what can it be attributed?

I believe that we are dealing with two substantially different modes of artistic expression. Proficiency in the visual arts must wait on development of the intellect. In painting, as in sculpture, concept is the basic element that then finds its expression in mastery of the media. Michelangelo has stated this best in one of his sonnets:

> Non ha l'ottimo artista alcun concetto c'un marmo solo in sè non circoscriva col suo soverchio; e solo a quello arriva la man che ubbidisce all'intelletto.
>
> (Not one single concept does the best artist have that a block of marble does not contain within itself covered by excess; and to that only arrives the hand that obeys the intellect.)

In contrast, music is strongly imbued with feeling. Its appeal and effect are essentially emotional. In children, the emotions dominate the still undeveloped intellect. Feeling is well and highly developed in the child long before the attainment of intellectual maturity during adolescence.

A note on encouraging creativity

Drawing a parallel with what has happened to African and Polynesian sculpture, Thévoz (1976) fears that current enthusiasm over child art may delay the child's progress in graphic representation.

"Primitive" art has lost most of its inspiration since its acceptance into the inner circle of great art. The same highly admired forms are being reproduced in great quantity as artists cater to the commercial art market and to the tourist trade.

Grown-ups often underestimate the astuteness of young children. Injudicious, excessive praise may cause the child to produce stereotyped replicas at the level of work that has been so enthusiastically admired, thereby preventing experimentation and delaying progress. I have repeatedly, in prior publications, warned against interference by adults, who with the best of intentions may be unaware of the harm they do with their questions, suggestions, and exaggerated praise (Di Leo, 1970).

Thévoz suggests that even the mentally ill may respond to the value attributed to their Art Brut by deliberately producing "lunatic art." At the same time, he laments the decline of creative faculty that has followed the widespread use of tranquillizers in the treatment of mental illness.

FIGURE 118

"Family singing" by Bill, age 8 years 7 months.

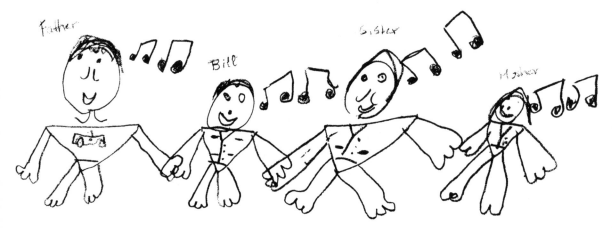

15

REFLECTIONS

As I write this concluding chapter, I have before me 97 human figure drawings by children from homes broken by poverty, disease, abuse, imprisonment, or abandonment. The children reside temporarily in group settings, pending transfer back to their own rehabilitated homes or into adoptive or foster homes. They are all latency-age children.

I am impressed first by the fact that 57 of the drawings show human figures that are tiny, repetitive, stereotyped so that it is difficult to distinguish one from the other (Figure 119). Twenty-two drawings depict family members at the bottom edge of the page. There is a preponderance of stick men in those drawn by boys, while those by girls are more complete though just as small (Figure 120). Such reduction in size and impoverishment of the figures are widely interpreted as expressions of insecurity and poor body image, as is the placement at the lower margin of the page for support.

In 42 kinetic-family-drawings by this group, both parents are represented in 27, even when there had actually been a single parent in the

FIGURE 119

Drawn by Charles, age 8 years. He drew
his two sisters; no parent figures.

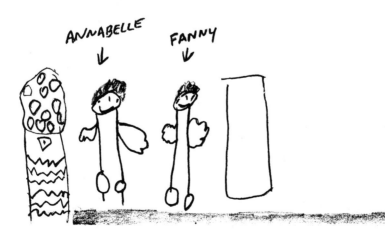

FIGURE 120

Drawn by Anabelle, age 12 years.

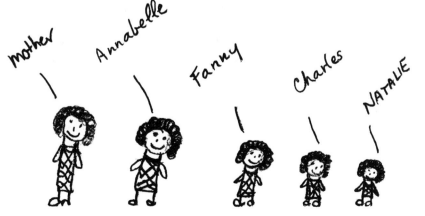

home (the mother in all but one instance). The attachment to siblings is strikingly evident by the inclusion of brothers and sisters in 36 of the 42 family drawings. Clearly, though the children are living apart from their parents, both are very much in their thoughts. But just as much, if not more, do the siblings represent a source of solidarity in their troubled world.

Only one angry child refused flatly and persistently to draw his family.

In marked contrast is Figure 121, drawn by Jane at age 4 years 8 months. She is living in her own intact, well-functioning family, the recipient of affectionate attention and intellectual stimulation. The pleasant family scene, the large figures freely and boldly drawn, the colorful costuming—all express the vivid fantasy and joie de vivre of an unfettered mind.

To the extent that familial-cultural-social factors can be modified and rendered favorable, prevention of psychological disorders and their behavioral manifestations will be correspondingly effective. Disruption of family life sets the stage for much maladjustment and unhappiness.

The children are telling us in pictorial language how they feel about themselves and the determining influences in their lives; how they need their parents. They are also telling that they need their siblings; that brothers and sisters must be together when placement into surrogate homes is the alternative. The drawings confirm what some of us have known through long familiarity with the effects of family disruption. It is no easy matter to place six related children into the same adoptive home. In any event, the relationship should be maintained even if separated placement is the only feasible solution.

There may be a good deal of rivalry and even fighting among siblings under ordinary conditions, but they will band together in adversity.

My approach to drawings has been typically clinical. I have tried to convey to the reader *ways of seeing*. I do not view the subject as a science, as that term is understood today. I can accept the term *science,* as applied to what we know about drawings, only in its original meaning derived from the Latin *scientia* from *scire* (to know).

Attempts to "elevate" the study of drawings to science (as systematized knowledge derived from observation, experimentation, and control) are laudable but as yet unconvincing. The validity of the conclusions derived therefrom, and of the scoring systems devised, remains questionable.

What need is there for a hundred similar cases and for statistical analysis when a boy, who is acting out aggressively since remarriage of his mother, draws himself with his natural father instead of with natu-

FIGURE 121

Drawn by Jane, age 4 years 3 months.

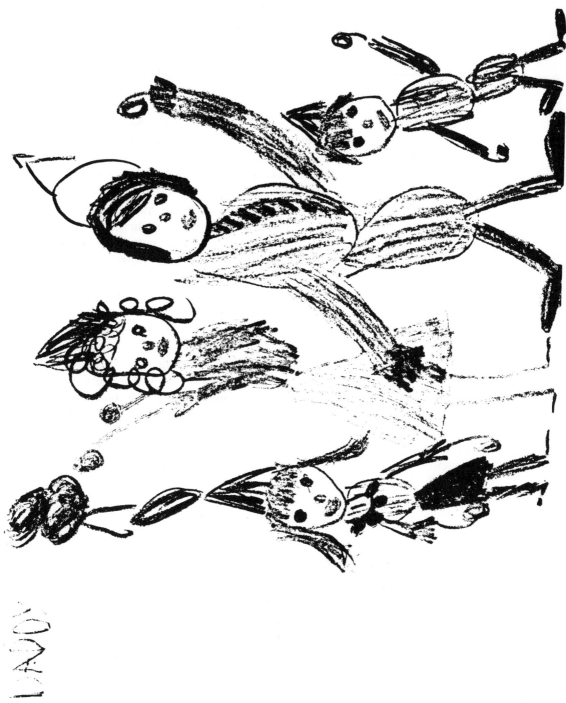

ral mother and new husband, the couple with whom he is actually residing? Is he not telling us clearly where he wants to be?

Validity and reliability and scientific objectivity are most desirable goals but there is also another way of reaching the heart of the matter. As I see it, an attempt to interpret child art within a single theoretical framework can only result in frustrating oversimplification.

More productive than a single-minded approach is an eclectic one that draws upon disciplines that have contributed significantly to our understanding of the infinite variety of human behavior. Statistical studies are valuable in revealing similarities and trends in drawing, as in other behavioral expression. But the methods of scientific investigation, impressively successful in the physical sciences, have not been able to penetrate the depths of personality that distinguish one individual from another so that no two are alike.

The study of individual differences in behavior will be more productive when it takes into account the significant contributions of the various disciplines that converge on human variety. Such an eclectic approach will draw upon neurophysiology, psychology in general and psychoanalysis in particular, education, and art. Even so, the knowledge thus obtained is but a part of the complex human reality. A multifaceted approach remains the only way past the tenacity with which the child within us resists the cultural pressures that would "split the knowledge from the dream" (Eiseley, 1978).

A great many studies have been directed at determining the validity of signs, symbols, and specific indicators, particularly those identified by Machover, despite her caution against losing sight of the first overall impression. I believe that research is more productive when aimed at the meaning of global features. Signs and specific indicators are most revealing when several are pointing in the same direction. How many? It is quality not quantity that counts. Some, like a smoking gun, are more blatant than others. The judgment of the examiner is indispensable. I do not see that person as being validly taken over by a machine.

Interpretation remains a basically subjective procedure. The reader may disagree with mine. Rather than dogmatic interpretations, they are offered in the spirit of a dialogue with the reader.

Having tried to make each chapter a unit and yet an integral part of the whole, "e pluribus unum," clarity without redundancy, I trust the reader will be tolerant where the effort has not been successful.

And lastly, mindful of Goethe's dictum that where an idea is wanting, a word can always be found to take its place, I have tried to avoid using the jargon of mine and allied professions.

Appendix

INTERPRETATION OF DRAWINGS: SUGGESTED PROCEDURE

(a) Global Impressions (holistic view):

spontaneous selection of subject
assigned topic

pleasant effect of the whole
unpleasant effect

drawn from memory
copied or imitating comic-strip character

freely drawn and bold
tiny and at bottom or well away from center

elaborate
limited

vivid fantasy
poor in content

own sex drawn first in D-A-P test
other sex drawn first

omission of self or other in family group
inclusion of all members

excessive shading
"artistic" shading for modeling of figure

static figures
movement indicated

full-face
profile

well coordinated figure
disjointed

symmetry
   preoccupation with perfect symmetry
   excessive disregard

quality of line
   broken
   continuous

pressure
   barely visible figure
   well defined
   heavy, may punch holes through paper

velocity
   speedy and careless
   exasperatingly slow

mood
   peaceful
   turbulent

organization
   orderly
   chaotic

composition
   simple
   complex

(b) Content (item analysis):

Human figure
  head
    huge
    disproportionately small

  eyes
    large
    small
    empty
    with pupils

  mouth
    absent or emphasized
    cosmetic or minimally represented

  arms
    large, muscular
    absent or stick-like

  legs
    two or more
    wide apart or close together

  crotch
    excessive attention, erasures
    shading, covered by hands

  trunk
    absent or tiny, smaller than head
    emphasized, organs or navel visible

  nose
    absent or tiny
    large, nostrils shown

  ears
    prominent
    absent

  hair
    abundant, coiffeured
    scribbled
    scant, absent

fingers
    five, supernumerary or absent
    stick or claw-like

breasts
    emphasized, firm or drooping
    absent

    genitalia
        suggested
        explicitly shown, exaggerated
        apparently ignored
        concealed

teeth
    large, pointed
    not visible

clothing
    appropriate
    incongruous
    profession or occupation shown
    scant or absent
    jewelry, ornaments

Bibliography

ALBERTI, L. B. *I Libri della Famiglia.* Translation by R. N. Watkins. Columbia, S. C.: University of South Carolina Press, 1969.

AMES, L. B. and ILG, F. L. The Gesell Incomplete Man Test as a measure of developmental status. *Genet. Psychol. Monog.,* 1965, 68:247–307.

ANASTASI, A. and FOLEY, J. P., JR. An analysis of spontaneous drawings by children in different cultures. *Jour. Appl. Psychol.,* 1936, 20:689–726.

ARIETI, S. *Creativity: The Magic Synthesis.* New York: Basic Books, 1976.

ARNHEIM, R. *Art and Visual Perception.* Berkeley and Los Angeles: University of California Press, 1964.

Arts, Education and Americans Panel. *Coming to our Senses.* New York: McGraw-Hill, 1977.

BARRON, F. The creative personality: Akin to madness. *Psychol. Today,* July 1972.

BENDER, L. The creative process in psycho-pathological art. *The Arts in Psychotherapy,* 1981, Vol. 8, No. 1.

BENDER, L. and WOLFSON, W. Q. The nautical theme in the art and fantasy of children. *Amer. J. Orthopsychiat.,* 1943, 13:436–467.

BERENSON, B. *Italian Painters of the Renaissance* (Preface). London: Phaidon, 1952.

BLAND, J. C. *Art of the Young Child.* New York: Museum of Modern Art, 1968.

BOLANDER, K. *Assessing Personality Through Tree Drawings.* New York: Basic Books, 1977.

BONINO, S., FONZI, A., and SAGLIONE, G. Sulla funzione dello spazio personale. *Età Evolutiva,* 1978, No. 1.

BRITSCH, G. *Theorie der Bildenen Kunst.* Munich: F. Bruckmann, 1926.

BROCA, P. Remarques sur la siège de la faculté de language articulé. Paris: *Bull. Soc. Anat.*, 1861, Sér.2,6:330–357.

BRUMBACK, R. A. Characteristics of the Inside-of-the-Body Test performed by normal school children. *Perceptual and Motor Skills*, 1977, 44:703–708.

BUCK, J. N. The H-T-P Test. *J. Clin. Psychol.*, 1948, 4:151–159.

BUCK, J. N. *The House-Tree-Person (H-T-P) Manual Supplement.* 4th printing. Beverly Hills, CA: Western Psychological Services, 1974.

BUDDHA. *Enciclopedia dell'Arte Antica.* Treccani. Roma: Istituto Poligrafico dell Stato, 1959.

BURNS, R. C. and KAUFMAN, S. H. *Kinetic Family Drawings (K-F-D): An Introduction to Understanding Children through Kinetic Drawings.* New York: Brunner/Mazel, 1970.

BURNS, R. C. and KAUFMAN, S. H. *Actions, Styles and Symbols in Kinetic Family Drawings.* New York: Brunner/Mazel, 1972.

CARDINAL, R. *Outsider Art.* New York: Praeger, 1972.

CHARBONNIER, G. *Conversations with Claude Lévi-Strauss.* London: Cape Editions, 1969.

CLAPARÈDE, E. *Psychologie de l'Enfant et Pédagogie Experimentale.* Paris: Delachaux et Nestlé, 1946.

CLARK, K. *The Drawings of Leonardo da Vinci.* 2nd ed. London: Phaidon, 1968.

COOMARASWAMY, A. K. *Elements of Buddhist Iconography.* Cambridge, MA: Harvard University Press, 1935.

COUSINS, N. Editorial. *Saturday Review*, Feb. 1981.

CRELIN, E. S. *Functional Anatomy of the Newborn.* New Haven: Yale University Press, 1973.

D'AMICO, V. Questions and answers about teaching art. In *Child Art: The Beginnings of Self-affirmation* (H. P. Lewis, Ed.). Berkeley: Diablo Press, 1973.

DAWSON, J. L. M. B. An anthropological perspective on the evolution and lateralization of the brain. In *Annals of New York Academy of Sciences.* New York: Vol. 299, 1977.

DÉCARIE, T. GOUIN. *Intelligence and Affectivity in Early Childhood.* New York: International Universities Press, 1965.

DENNIS, W. *Group Values through Children's Drawings.* New York: J. Wiley, 1966.

DESPERT, J. L. *The Inner Voices of Children.* New York: Simon and Schuster, 1973.

DI LEO, J. H. *Young Children and their Drawings.* New York: Brunner/Mazel, 1970.

DI LEO, J. H. *Children's Drawings as Diagnostic Aids.* New York: Brunner/Mazel, 1973.

DI LEO, J. H. *Child Development: Analysis and Synthesis.* New York: Brunner/Mazel, 1977.

DI LEO, J. H. Graphic activity of young children: Development and creativity. In *Art: Basic for Young Children.* (L. Lasky and R. Mukerji, Eds.) Washington: National Association for Education of Young Children, 1980.

ENG, H. *The Psychology of Children's Drawings.* (2nd ed.) London: Routledge and Kegan Paul, 1954.

EISELEY, L. *The Star Thrower.* New York: Times Books, 1978.

EISNER, E. W. Building curricula for art education. In *Aesthetics and Problems of Education* (R. A. Smith, ed.). Urbana, IL: University of Illinois Press, 1971.

ERIKSON, E. H. *Childhood and Society.* New York: Norton, 1950.

FRAIBERG, S. H. *The Magic Years.* New York: Scribner's, 1959.

FREEMAN, N. How young children try to plan drawings. In *The Child's Representation of the World* (G. Butterworth, Ed.). New York: Plenum Press, 1977.

FREUD, A. *Normality and Pathology in Childhood.* New York: International Universities Press, 1965.

FREUD, S. *A General Introduction to Psychoanalysis.* New York: Doubleday, Garden City, 1943.

FREUD, S. *The Interpretation of Dreams*. New York: Basic Books, 1958.

GARDNER, H. *The Arts and Human Development*. New York: J. Wiley, 1973.

GARDNER, H. *Artful Scribbles*. New York: Basic Books, 1980.

GESELL, A. and AMATRUDA, C. S. *Developmental Diagnosis*. New York: Paul B. Hoeber, 1941.

GESELL, A., ILG, F. L., and AMES, L. B. *Infant and Child in the Culture of Today*. New York: Harper and Row, 1974.

GIANI GALLINO, T. *Il Complesso di Laio: I Rapporti Famigliari nei Disegni dei Ragazzi*. Torino: Einaudi, 1977.

GOMBRICH, E. H. *Art and Illusion*. Princeton: Princeton University Press, 1972.

GOODENOUGH, F. L. *Measurement of Intelligence by Drawings*. New York: World Book Co., 1926.

GRIFFITH, A. V. and PEYMAN, D. A. R. Eye-ear emphasis in the draw-a-person test as indicating ideas of reference. In *Handbook of Projective Techniques* (B. L. Murstein, Ed.). New York: Basic Books, 1965.

GRIFFITHS, R. *A Study of Imagination in Early Childhood*. London: Routledge and Kegan Paul, 1946.

GUARDO, C. J. Personal space in children. *Child Devel.*, 1969, 40:143–151.

HAITH, M. M., MOORE, M. J., and BERGMAN, T. Eye contact and face scanning in early infancy. *Science*, 1977, 198:853–855.

HALBREICH, U. Drawings of cephalopodes by schizophrenic patients, and their meaning. In *Art Psychotherapy*, 1979, 6:18–23.

HAMMER, E. F. *The Clinical Application of Projective Drawings*. Springfield, IL: Charles C Thomas, 1967.

HAMMER, E. F. Hierarchical organization of personality and the H-T-P achromatic and chromatic. In *Advances in the House-Tree-Person Technique: Variations and Applications* (J. N. Buck and E. F. Hammer, Eds.). Los Angeles: Western Psychol. Services, 1969.

HARRIS, D. B. *Children's Drawings as Measures of Intellectual Maturity*. New York: Harcourt, Brace and World, 1963.

HARRIS, D. B., ROBERTS, J., and PINDER, G. D. *Intellectual Maturity of Children as Measured by the Goodenough-Harris Drawing Test*. National Center for Health Statistics. Series II, No. 105. Washington, D.C.: U.S. Dept. of Health, Education, and Welfare, December 1970.

HAUSER, S. T. *Black and White Identity Formation*. New York: Wiley-Interscience, 1971.

HESS, E. H. *Imprinting*. New York: Van Nostrand Reinhold, 1973.

HOROWITZ, B. L., LEWIS, H., and LUCA, M. *Understanding Children's Art for Better Teaching*. (2nd ed.) Columbus, OH: C. E. Merrill, 1973.

HUTT, C. Cerebral asymmetry and hemispheric specialization: Some implications of sex differences. In *International J. Behavioral Devel.*, 2(1):73–87, Amsterdam, March 1979.

HUXLEY, A. *The Human Situation*. New York: Harper and Row, 1977.

HUXLEY, J. Introduction to Teilhard de Chardin's *The Phenomenon of Man*. New York: Harper and Row, 1961.

JOHNSON, J. H. Note on the validity of Machover's indicators of anxiety. *Perceptual and Motor Skills*, August 1971, 33(1):126.

JOURDAIN, F. L'art et l'enfant. *Le Point. Revue Artistique et Litteraire*, 9–19. Mulhouse, France, Juillet 1953.

JUNG, C. G. *Man and His Symbols*. New York: Doubleday, 1964.

JUNG, C. G. *Analytical Psychology: Its Theory and Practice*. London: Routledge and Kegan Paul, 1968.

KARP, S. A. and MARLENS, H. Field dependence in relation to miniature toys play. Unpublished study.

KATZAROFF, M. D. Qu'est-ce que les enfants dessinent? *Arch. de Psychologie*, 1909–1910, 9:125–233.

Kay, P. Psychoanalytic theory of development in childhood and preadolescence. In *Handbook of Child Psycho-analysis* (B. B. Wolman, Ed.). New York: Van Nostrand Reinhold, 1972.

Kay, S. R. Qualitative differences in human figure drawings according to schizophrenic subtype. *Perceptual and Motor Skills*, 1978, 47:923–932.

Kellog, R. and O'Dell, S. *The Psychology of Children's Art.* New York: Random House, 1967.

Kerschensteiner, D. G. *Die Entwicklung der Zeichnerischen Begabung.* Munich: Gerber, 1905.

Klee, F. *Paul Klee.* Zurich: Diogenes, 1963.

Klepsch, M. and Logie, L. *Children Draw and Tell.* New York: Brunner/Mazel, 1982.

Koch, K. *Der Baumtest.* Bern: H. Huber, 1949.

Lansing, K. M. *Art, Artists and Art Education.* New York: McGraw-Hill, 1969.

Levinstein, S. *Kinderzeichnungen bis zum 14 Lebensjahr.* Leipzig: R. Voigtlander Verlag, 1905.

Levy, J. Possible basis for the evolution of lateral specialization of the human brain. *Nature*, 1969, 224:614–615.

Levy, J. The mammalian brain and the adaptive advantage of cerebral asymmetry. *Annals of New York Academy of Sciences.* Vol. 229, 1977.

Lewis, H. P. (Ed.) *Child Art: The Beginnings of Self-affirmation.* Berkeley: Diablo Press, 1973.

Lowenfeld, V. and Brittain, W. L. *Creative and Mental Growth.* New York: Macmillan, 1975.

Luquet, G. H. *Les Dessins d'un Enfant: Étude Psychologique.* Paris: Librairie Felix Alcan, 1913.

Machover, K. *Personality Projection in the Drawing of the Human Figure.* Springfield, IL: Charles C Thomas, 1949.

Maitland, L. What children draw to please themselves. *Inland Educator,* 1895, Vol. 1.

McHugh, A. F. Children's figure drawings in neurotic and conduct disturbances. *J. Clin. Psychol.,* 1966, 22:219–221.

Mishima, Y. *Spring Snow.* New York: A. A. Knopf, 1972.

Money, J., Hampson, J. G., and Hampson, J. L. Imprinting and the establishment of gender-role. *Arch. Neurol. and Psychiat.,* 1957, 77:333.

Mühle, G. *Entwicklungspsychologie des Zeichnerischen Gestaltens.* Munich: J. A. Barth, 1955.

Morino Abbele, F. *Interpretazioni Psicologiche del Disegno Infantile.* Firenze: Edizioni OS, 1970.

Muschoot, F. and Demeyer, W. *Le Teste du Dessin d'un Arbre.* Brussels: Editest, 1974.

Naumberg, M. Studies of the "free" art expression of behavior problem children and adolescents as a means of diagnosis and therapy. *Nerv. Mental Dis. Monograph,* No. 71. New York: Coolidge Foundation, 1947.

Oppenheimer, J. M. Studies of brain asymmetry: Historical perspective. In Evolution and lateralization of the Brain (S. J. Diamond and D. A. Blizard, Eds.). *Annals of New York Academy of Sciences.* New York: Vol. 299:4–18, 1977.

Ornstein, R. *The Psychology of Consciousness.* San Francisco: W. H. Freeman, 1975.

Partridge, L. Children's drawings of men and women. *Studies in Education* (E. Barnes, Ed.). 1902, 2:163–179.

Petrarca, F. *Canzoniere.* CVI. Novara: I.G.D.A., 1962.

Piaget, J. *The Construction of Reality in the Child.* New York: Basic Books, 1954.

Piaget, J. *The Language and Thought of the Child.* Cleveland: World Publ. Co., 1955.

Piaget, J. and Inhelder, B. *Mental Imagery in the Child.* New York: Basic Books, 1971.

Proust, M. *Swann's Way* and *Within a Budding Grove.* New York: Vintage Books, 1970.

Prudhommeau, N. *Le Dessin de l'Enfant.* Paris: Presse Universitaire de France, 1947.

Pulaski, A. S. *Understanding Piaget.* New York: Harper and Row, 1971.

Read, H. *Art and Society.* New York: Schocken Books, 1966.

Ricci, C. *L'Arte dei Bambini.* Bologna: Zanichelli, 1887.

ROBBINS, A. and SIBLEY, L. B. *Creative Art Therapy.* New York: Brunner/Mazel, 1976.

RORSCHACH, H. *Psychodiagnostics.* Bern: Verlag Hans Huber, 1942.

RUSSELL, E. R. Measurement of intelligence by means of children's drawings. *Amer. J. Art Therapy,* July 1979, Vol. 18.

SCHILDER, P. *The Image and Appearance of the Human Body.* New York: International Universities Press, 1950.

SCOTT, J. P. The process of primary socialization in canine and human infants. *Soc. Research Ch. Devel.,* 1963, Monograph No. 85, Vol. 28.

SOMMER, R. *Personal Space.* Englewood Cliffs, N.J.: Prentice-Hall, 1969.

SHAKESPEARE, W. *The Tempest.* Act II, Scene 1.

STENT, G. Thinking about seeing. *The Sciences,* May/June 1980, Vol. 20, No. 5.

STRATTON, L. C., TEKIPPE, D. J., and FLICK. G. L. Personal space and self-concept. *Sociometry,* 1973, 36(3):424–429.

SWENSON, C. H. Empirical evaluation of human figure drawings: 1957–1966. *Psychol. Bull.,* 1968, 70:20–24.

TAYLOR, I. A. The nature of the creative process. In *Creativity—An Examination of the Creative Process* (P. Smith, Ed.). New York: Hastings House, 1959.

THÉVOZ, M. *Art Brut.* New York: Rizzoli, 1976.

TREVOR-ROPER, P. *The World through Stunted Sight.* New York: Bobbs-Merrill, 1970.

U.S. Department of Health, Education and Welfare. Central processing dysfunction in children: A review of research. *NINDS Monograph* No. 9, 1969.

WINNICOTT, D. W. *Therapeutic Consultations in Child Psychiatry.* New York: Basic Books, 1971.

WITKIN, H. A., LEWIS, H. B., HERTZMAN, M., MACHOVER, K., MEISSNER, P. E., and WAPNER, S. *Personality through Perception.* New York: Harper, 1954.

WITKIN, H. A., DYK, R. B., FATERSON, H. F., GOODENOUGH, D. R., and KARP, S. A. *Psychological Differentiation.* New York: J. Wiley, 1962.

WOLFF, W. The personality of the preschool child. New York: Grune and Stratton, 1946.

WÖLFLI, A. *Catalogue of Works by Adolf Wölfli* (B. Spoerri and J. Glaesemer, Eds.). Berne: Adolf Wölfli Foundation, Museum Fine Arts, 1976.

ZAZZO, R. Le geste graphique et la structuration de l'espace. *Enfance,* 1950, 3–4:202–240.

ZAZZO, R. La genèse de la conscience de soi. *Psychologie de la Connaissance de Soi.* Paris: P.U.F., 1975.

INDEX OF NAMES

INDEX OF SUBJECTS

India, 13
Inside-of-the-Body test, 123
Integration of body parts, 24–26, 202
Interpretation, 3–16
    clinical approach to, 3–4
    developmental perspective on, 5–11
    role of speech in, 4–5
    statistical analysis in, 3–4, 216
    symbols in. See Symbols
    use of space in. See Space
Inversion, 20–21
Isolation in family drawings, 72

Kinetic Family Drawing (K-F-D), 74,
    134–36

Latency, viii
    sex differences and, 132–33
Laterality, 146–66
    cognitive style in:
        body image in drawings and,
            164–66
        handedness and, 163–64
        perception and, 164
    directionality and profile orienta-
        tion, 148–49, 158
    early effect of handedness on, 146
    eye and hand coordination in, 146–
        48
    handedness detected from drawings,
        149–57
    hemisphere specialization and, 163
    reversal of letters and numbers and,
        158–61
    right-left handedness and, 162–63
Line, quality of, 17–19, 28–29

Mandala, 13
Mental retardation, drawing and,
    176–79
Minimalism, 65–66
Minnesota Multiphasic Personality
    Inventory, 188
Mothers, absent, 96–98
Movement:
    depiction of, 89–91
    illusion of, 86–89
Music, 209–10

Perception:
    cognitive style and, 164
    of sex differences:
        in preschoolers. 127–29

in school-age children, 130–31
Personality:
    projection of, in drawings, 59–60
    tree drawings and, 167–74
Perspective, 50
Placement, 13–16
Profiles, handedness and, 148–49,
    158
Projection, 59–74
    cognitive-affective ratio and, 69–71
    of emotion in child art, 60–64
    in family drawings, 72–75
    in House-Tree-Person Test, 41–44
    minimalism and stereotypy in draw-
        ings, 65–66
    personal space and, 66–68
Psychodiagnostics (Rorschach), 5

Rapport, 4
Realism, visual versus intellectual, 31,
    37–38, 46–51
Rod-and-Frame tests (RFT), 164, 165

Schizophrenia, 188–89
    Art Brut and, 190–92, 210
    distinguishing of, in drawings, 192–
        94
Science, in drawing interpretation, 85
Scribbling, handedness and, 149–53
Self:
    drawing as image of, 104–106
    omission of, in family drawings, 72,
        94–95
Self-esteem, personal space and, 66–68
Serial specimens:
    inconsistency and, 195–98
    symbols in, 12
Sex differences:
    latency and, 132–33
    preschool perceptions of, 127–29
    school-age children and, 130–31
Sex roles:
    in drawings of emotionally disturbed
        children, 185–87
    emancipation of women and, 141–
        45
    placement of drawings and, 14
    school-age children and, 130–31
    sex drawn first and, 92–93
    in western society, 134–41
Sexuality:
    latency and, viii
    symbols for, 12–13